Ebb and Flow

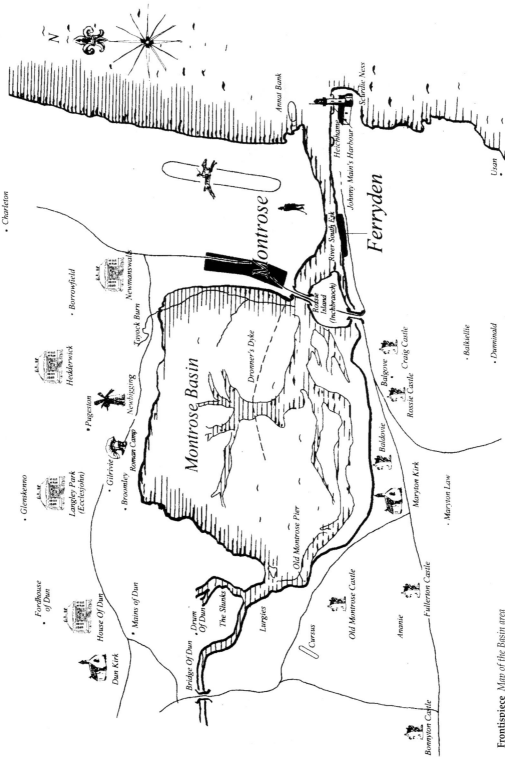

Frontispiece *Map of the Basin area*

Ebb and Flow

Aspects of
the History of
Montrose Basin

Montrose Basin Heritage Society

The Pinkfoot Press
Balgavies, Angus
2004

Published 2004 in Scotland by
The Pinkfoot Press
Balgavies, Forfar, Angus DD8 2TH
on behalf of
Montrose Basin Heritage Society

ISBN 1 874012 45 8

This volume is published with the help of a grant from The Heritage Lottery Fund

Front cover
Winter Sunrise over Montrose Basin (photograph: D Macdonald)

Typeset and designed at The Pinkfoot Press
Printed by The Cromwell Press, Trowbridge

This book
is dedicated to the late

Archie McCallum

a tireless worker for
Montrose Basin Wildlife Centre
and a keen historical researcher
on all to do with Montrose
and the surrounding area

Contents

List of Illustrations

Illustration Acknowledgements

The contributors are very grateful to the following organisations and individuals who have kindly permitted reproduction of their copyright material:

a3francke, Veere, The Netherlands (**39**); Alasdair Macdonald (**6**); Angus Council Cultural Services (**5, 7–9, 12, 19–20, 46–49**); Caledonian Maps (**1, 4**); Neil Werninck (**10**); Penrose Lindsay (**38, 40, 43**); The Frick Collection, New York (**30–31**); The Stewartry Museum, Kirkcudbright (**36**); The Royal Commission on the Ancient and Historical Monuments of Scotland (RCAHMS) (**28–29**).

The drawings and maps (**Frontispiece, 11, 16–18, 21–23, 25, 27, 32–34, 37, 44**) are by David Parker.

Acknowledgements

The authors would like to acknowledge the support of many people in the writing of this book. Our principal thanks must go to the Heritage Lottery Fund (Awards for All) whose generous grant made it possible for this book to be published, to Angus Council for allowing the use of a number of William Lamb's etchings and ink drawings, and to Dennis Rice who most helpfully edited a draft of the book. We are very grateful to the staff of the Scottish Wildlife Trust, particularly those of the Montrose Basin Wildlife Centre, who probably never envisaged quite this outcome when they suggested a survey of the history and archaeology of Montrose Basin. The members of the Montrose Basin Heritage Society (and the Tuesday Group) who do not have chapters here, but have nevertheless provided necessary information and support, deserve our thanks: they include Andy Wakelin, Ian Hargreaves, Kip and Hilda Fraser, Anne Hardcastle, Henrietta Somervell, Virginia Fraser, Ann Wyllie, and the late Archie MacCallum. Essential information was provided by Angus Council. In particular, thanks go to Fiona Scharlau and her indefatigable team – Ruth Parsonson, Heather Munro, and Sheila Simpson at Angus Local Studies Centre in Montrose, and the staff at Forfar Library. But especial mention must be made of the Montrose Museum and staff: Rachel Benvie, Linda Fraser, Louise Clark and Joan MacLaren, who not only provided a meeting place for the group, but also provided constant help and support. The Royal Commission on the Ancient and Historical Monuments of Scotland and the Aberdeenshire Council Archaeology Service both provided information (from the National Monuments Record and the Angus Sites and Monuments Record). Scottish National Heritage (Airlie office) kindly allowed access to their aerial photographic coverage. Material was also provided by Historic Scotland and by the National Archives of Scotland, Edinburgh. Landowners who kindly allowed us access to their land were: Mr & Mrs Fraser, West Mains of Rossie; Harry Fleming, Old Montrose; Willie Lawrie, Maryton; Ian Hourston, Drum; George Luke and Philip Santer, Langley Park; The Earl of Southesk, who very helpfully provided access to his private archives on a number of occasions. Our thanks also go to all the local people who have provided information, especially Mrs Jane Stewart and Mrs Priscilla Sharp. Particular thanks are offered for help with individual chapters: For the Time Line to Graham and Margaret King and Jonathan Fraser. For the chapter on Place-names to the late David Dorward, Norman Atkinson, John Ogilvie and Ian Shirlaw. For the chapter on Erskine of Dun to Wendy McDonald and Douglas Lamb. For the chapter on Langley Park to Professor Michael Moss, the late Brigadier John Knox, Dr Simon Martin and Mrs Dorothy Bruce-Gardyne. For the chapters on Salmon Fishing and Mussel Cultivation to Willie Shearer, Penrose Lindsay, Ingrid Thomson, Bill Crowe, Norman Atkinson, W F Ogg, Ian Shirlaw, Adri Franke, and David Mitchell (SNH). But our most grateful thanks must go to our families, who had to put up with a great deal during the gestation of this work.

Foreword

Montrose Basin is a truly magical place. I first discovered its charms in December 1962 when the Dundee Branch of the Scottish Ornithologists' Club arranged an outing to Montrose Basin and Scurdie Ness. Many visits followed, initially on my trusty Raleigh bicycle, and a life-long relationship began.

While I was certainly on the receiving end of this partnership to begin with, I was delighted to get the chance to do something in return. In 1976, Bernard Gilchrist, the then Secretary of the comparatively young Scottish Wildlife Trust telephoned me. The Angus Branch of the Trust, of which I was a committee member, had just purchased Balgavies Loch, and now we were being offered the chance to purchase Montrose Basin for a mere £28,000. I spent the rest of the conversation waxing lyrical about the Basin, Bernard was convinced and we subsequently bought it.

Owning the Basin was one thing, however, but giving it much needed protection and investment was another. We brought Angus District Council on board in order to achieve a Local Nature Reserve Agreement. By that time I had joined the District Council as an employee, so with a foot in each camp I became the first secretary of the Montrose Basin Local Nature Reserve Committee!

During the early 1980s this was achieved, and I thoroughly enjoyed all the work which got the Basin the protection it needed. One important sub-committee during this period began to gather much needed information on the Basin, and not just its wildlife. Long after I had moved on, I was delighted to see the formation of the Montrose Basin Heritage Society, which really advanced this work.

This publication is the result of much of these efforts, and what a fascinating read it makes! The authors of each chapter must be congratulated on their hard work, not only with the research, but also in making each contribution so readable.

I hope that this publication will be the starting point for researchers in the future, and I trust it will be their inspiration. Even if readers do not have such lofty aims, I sincerely hope that they enjoy reading these chapters, and that locals therefore take pride in the Basin – this wonderful asset on their doorstep. To those who do not have the good fortune to live by its shores, whether from Auchmithie or Auckland, then I hope that once you have read this that the first thing you must do is visit!

Norman Atkinson
Head of Cultural Services, Angus Council
August 2004

The Contributors

Hilary White, a professional archaeologist, arrived in Montrose in December 1998 for a six-month stay. She is still in town (part-time) and enjoying researching the history of the area.

Linda Fraser is originally from Orkney. She and her family settled in Angus in 1990. She works part-time in Montrose Museum and apart from amateur history interests she spends most of her time in her cottage garden battling the weeds.

Duncan Macdonald spent almost 30 years as a dental practitioner in the town, and retired at 'the turn of the century'. He now pursues an interest in local history, among other ploys.

Forbes Inglis is a freelance writer and local historian whose work appears regularly in magazines and in the *Montrose Review*. His best-selling novel is proceeding at a pace similar to the erection of the Scottish Parliament building.

Amanda Briant-Evans studied history at Somerville College, Oxford. She and her family have lived in the Montrose area since 1980. She was involved in the historical research for the opening of the House of Dun in 1989, and now works there as a guide.

Graham King studied Geology at the Universities of Glasgow and Manchester. He was formerly Curator of Museum Services, Moray District, and Keeper of Collections, Dundee Industrial Heritage.

David Parker, house-husband, dog-walker, and part-time artist, joined Montrose Basin Heritage Society to assist with illustration.

Introduction

This book grew out of a decision in 1999 to undertake a wide-ranging survey of the Montrose Basin area. The Basin has been designated both a 'Site of Special Scientific Interest' (SSSI) and a RAMSAR (internationally important wetland) site. In view of the national importance of the area, the Scottish Wildlife Trust runs a visitor centre located on its southern shore. A management plan for the Local Nature Reserve suggested that a more intensive study of the area and its significance should be implemented. The survey was to be carried out by local volunteers. Themed topics for study were identified covering both the natural and man-made heritage interests. It rapidly became apparent that, just as the 'green' interests were of national importance, so much of man's impact on the area was of major archaeological and historic interest as well.

A small group of local volunteers, dubbed the 'Tuesday Group', started to assess existing information on the history of the Basin area. Primary and secondary written sources, historic maps, illustrations, photographs, finds in museums, and a number of sites were checked. A clearer picture is now emerging of the Basin at various periods in the past. In addition a number of buildings and estate centres have been researched in increasing depth.

The focus of the survey is the area of the parishes surrounding the Basin. The Town of Montrose, while obviously the dominating influence of the area, has been extensively studied, and is not essentially part of the inquiry. Because of the importance of Montrose and its surrounding area in the past, research of this type can take many lifetimes. This book aims to present just a small fraction of what has been revealed by this research to date. Individual members of the Tuesday Group have taken topics that have particularly interested them during the wider Basin Survey and present some of their results in this book.

1 *Detail from* County Map of Forfarshire *(A & C Black, 1847) showing the surrounding parishes. (Caledonian Maps –* www.caledonianmaps.co.uk)

1 Setting the Scene

Montrose lies at the eastern end of the South Esk River where it flows into the North Sea. Once a broad estuary, the access to the sea has been partly reduced by a spit of land laid down from the northern side of the river. Montrose town now lies on this spit, with its medieval core located on the highest point. The floor of the South Esk valley is relatively flat for some way upstream and, as the South Esk is tidal for nearly three kilometres inland, the area to the west of the town floods creating a large lagoon of relatively shallow salt water. When the tide recedes most of the area remains as open mud-flats cut by the channels of the South Esk and other smaller watercourses.

The depth and shape of the Basin has altered over the millennia and aerial photographs clearly show that the course of the River South Esk has shifted as well. There have been a number of attempts to drain and reclaim portions of the Basin since the seventeenth century, some having more permanent results than others. Historical documents also point to the erosion that has occurred closer to the mouth of the river and the measures to prevent this, not least to save the important area now occupied by the docks. There are claims that the port area once extended much further to the south, into what is now the river channel and that it was almost possible 'to shake hands with people on Rossie Island'. More graphically, we are also told that in the nineteenth century (after the first bridges had been built) the sites of old wells were visible in the northern channel. Both river channels have been bridged since 1799 for road access and then in the 1860s for the railway. The latter was perhaps more drastic, with 'the Scaup' – a large gravel bank and mussel bed off the north side of Rossie Island – being removed to provide the material to embank the railway line to the north, when finds from several early shipwrecks were recovered. More recently still, the southern channel of the South Esk has been infilled to link Rossie Island and Ferryden and increase the harbour area.

Parishes around the Basin

There are currently four parishes that surround the Basin – Montrose and Dun on the north side of the South Esk River, and Maryton and Craig on the south side. These incorporate two more that we know about – Ecclesjohn (or Egglisjohn), which lay between Montrose and Dun, and Dunninald, which lay within the southern portion of the now enlarged Craig parish. However, the parishes' extent was probably much more complex in earlier periods, apparently based on estates that allowed utilisation of a broader range of land types – good agricultural land, poorer upland grazing, access to the coastline, and access to the Basin itself. The parishes would have been gradually consolidated to what we see today. The archaeological and historical survey research area has been largely concentrated on these modern parishes.

Montrose

Montrose parish lies on the north east side of the Basin adjacent to the sea. The Royal Burgh, originally of Sallork or Cellurca, but now Montrose, lies within this. The Burgh was previously surrounded by its 'town lands'. These formed a limited portion of the wider parish, whose western edge was formed by the bounds of Montrose Muir and the Tayock Burn (its exact extent is not now clear). The Royal Burgh has all the appearances of a deliberately 'planned' settlement, with regular-sized property holdings set around a central market place immediately north of the royal castle. It is likely that this area of the town was laid out in the twelfth century. It lies to the north of the main port area, which was called Stromnay until the fifteenth century. This name, together with the '-gait' elements of the local streets – Seagait and Castlegait – clearly indicates that some form of settlement here was established by the Norse period, and possibly several centuries earlier. The burgh inevitably dominated the parish, but smaller estate centres at Newmanswalls, Charleton and Borrowfield lay to the north and are documented throughout both the medieval and post-medieval periods.

Ecclesjohn

The full extent of the parish of Ecclesjohn, or Egglisjohn, has never been determined. The parish was amalgamated with Dun in 1583. Earlier estate records for much of the area are lacking. The name Egglis / Eccles – meaning church – undoubtedly refers to an early chapel site that is described as a place of pilgrimage, but was ruinous by the sixteenth century. The tenant for much of the medieval period was the Cathedral at Brechin. But by the first decade of the fifteenth century there were legal disputes as to the lordship of the estate, with the Erskines of Dun challenging what the church believed were their ancient rights. Ultimately a compromise was reached with Brechin accepting the overlordship of Dun in exchange for paying a token rent. The name Ecclesjohn was retained until the eighteenth century when the main estate was renamed Langley Park. But two other estates, Tayock and Hedderwick to the east, have now largely disappeared. Tayock Mill still survives on the Tayock Burn to the east of the old house site. The walled garden at Hedderwick survives in part, but in 1984 the remaining walls of the ruined house were demolished and limited photographs now form the main record of what it looked like.

Dun

Dun parish lies on the north-western edge of Montrose Basin, although it had a strange small outlying section surrounded by Montrose, in an area now covered by the Royal Infirmary, until the nineteenth century. Dun has been described as one of the most important baronies in Scotland. John de Hastings received the Barony of Dun from William the Lion in the twelfth century, and it passed to the Erskine family about two hundred years later. They controlled the whole parish, and appear to have been the family who held their lands the longest in continuous occupation – over six centuries. The name 'Dun' reflects the antiquity of the area and suggests that there was once a defended fort site here guarding the north side of the river crossing, perhaps as early as the prehistoric period. It is possible that it lay on the west side of the Den of Dun on the outcrop where the medieval castle once lay, or if larger, it could have lain on the higher ground to the north. By the seventeenth century the castle site had been shifted to the east of the Den of Dun, and the eighteenth-century House of Dun (now owned by National Trust for Scotland) lies close to its site. The dominance of the Erskines throughout much of the medieval and post-medieval periods did not allow rival estates to grow in the parish, although at times some of the major farms would be used as dower houses, indicating they might well have been of some importance. Some farms such as Balwyllo, Balnillo and Mains of Dun are survivors on much earlier sites. Broomley apparently was improved and its grounds laid out in the eighteenth century.

MARYTON

Maryton, which lies at the south-western edge of the Basin, is the other parish that must derive its name from the early chapel that lay within it. The history of the various estates that lay within the parish is very complex. Additionally, income from the parish was granted to Restenneth Priory ('a teind of the salt works of Munros'), and then in 1178 King William the Lion conferred Maryton Parish on the newly-founded Arbroath Abbey. The main estate was undoubtedly the royal one at Old Montrose. This perhaps developed to control the southern side of the river crossing. It appears that from the twelfth century at the latest, it had a special relationship with the Burgh, which not only changed its name to Montrose, but also possibly had important facilities such as mills and salt pans here. In 1325, Robert the Bruce, not a frequent visitor to the estate like some of his predecessors, exchanged it for Cardross with the Graham family, who held it until the latter part of the seventeenth century. Another estate centre with a castle site lay at Bonnyton. Bonnyton was vested in the hands of the hereditary keepers of the Kings Forest at Montreathmont – the Tulloch and then the Wood families. Between these two estates lay the lost estate of Annanie. A little to the east lay the lesser estate of Fullerton; this tenancy was vested in the hands of the King's hereditary fowlers – a family designated 'de Fullerton'.

CRAIG

Craig, meaning rock, lies on the south-eastern edge of the Basin and on the south side of the South Esk. Its full extent before its amalgamation with Dunninald (also known as St Skea), is not known, but the island of Inchbrayoch (Rossie) lay within it. The chapel here, perhaps first established as early as the seventh or eighth century AD, became the parish church. Craig was also an estate centre with its own castle – the current Craig House. Another estate was centred on Rossie, again with its own castle and important water mills. The farm now called West Mains of Rossie apparently had its own castle and water mill. Further research is needed to check this area to determine its early history. For much of the post-medieval period the two estates of Craig and Rossie were held in common. One or other house/castle would form the primary residence and the other would be the dower house (or equivalent). Rossie came to final prominence with the building of a spectacular mansion house with designed grounds in about 1800 at the then considerable sum of £30,000. But less than a century later the owners had moved out and the house was demolished in the 1950s, having been derelict and roofless for some time. Another smaller estate, but again with its own castle, was Baldovie, home in the sixteenth century to the Melville family. This lay closer to the Basin, probably on an earlier Pictish site. Balgove, allegedly the site of an ancient prison, also lay within the parish.

DUNNINALD

The history of Dunninald requires more study, but it was an early parish with its own church of St Skeoch, or Skae, close to the coast. The parish was amalgamated into Craig in the sixteenth-century Reformation. The bounds of the early parish have not been determined, but it is known from documentary sources that it also had its own castle. Its location has still not been confirmed. One antiquarian tradition hints that this lay in the north part of the parish where it overlooked the River South Esk, but several other sites have also been suggested. In part of the post-medieval period the estate of Usan ran with Rossie in Craig, but by the eighteenth century it had its own 'big house', which still survives. The parish system was, of course, created in the medieval period and overlay a much older structure of settlement. But it is clear that for much of the period of human development, the area around the Basin would have been covered with a series of farmsteads of greater or lesser size. These would have exploited the better agricultural land at the lower levels of the valley for arable farming, or possibly water meadows for grazing and used the more upland areas for rough grazing and for quarrying and fuel sources. It is noticeable that the main farm sites tend to lie above the older flood levels of the River South Esk. There is a strong possibility that many farm sites could have been established for over a thousand years.

THE PORT

It is not clear exactly when a port centre developed at the mouth of the River South Esk. Its early name Stromnay, of Norse origin, indicates it is likely to have been established by the ninth century at the latest, but it is possible that (in some form) it could have been considerably older. Early antiquarian reports claim that Viking invaders burned Montrose (or its early equivalent) at least once, but as yet there is no conclusive proof of this. Nevertheless the area was chosen for the establishment of a Royal Burgh, probably in the twelfth century. A burgh when formed has a special legal status, and royal burghs were established to provide income to the crown, to control taxes, but also to provide a centre for the operating of royal policies. Major tenants, or burgers, would pay enhanced rents, but in exchange they had free toll within the Burgh markets. All foreign exports, such as salmon, hides and woolfells, had to be exported through a Royal Burgh, which was certainly advantageous for the burgers. By becoming the most important regional market, Montrose could attract more custom allowing a broader range of industries to flourish in the town and new classes of goods to be traded. Thus the town would grow in spite of several vicissitudes, such as invasion and fire. By the fourteenth century Montrose was one of the richest ports in Scotland.

The Castle

The establishment of a royal castle on the burgh boundary would usually lead to greater safety for the town, but would also ensure the more regular presence of the monarch and the courtiers. It would be important that the nearby estates were in the hands of loyal tenants – in the early period many of these would be families of Norman descent. In addition, it seems that a number of estates around the Basin were directly linked to the provision of services to the crown. Fullerton and Bonnyton have already been mentioned; Usan had to provide fish for the royal court when the King was at Forfar; while others had to provide provisions to the royal castle at Montrose. However, because there were marked financial benefits attached to owning a house with burgage rights in the town, a number of local landowners with estates in the area also had a town house. These could be used at various times of the year to support business, or trading activities for example, or more simply just to provide a better social life. The defensive role of the town would gradually have decreased as Scotland became more stable and the castle reverted to a private residence.

Maps and Documents

Analysis of documentary and cartographic evidence available allows us to build a more detailed picture of the area and its individual sites in the post-medieval period and to a lesser extent in the medieval period. For undocumented periods we have to rely on a range of other information sources. These sources might be finds or excavated material, evidence from aerial photography, or place-names. Information of this type is not so readily available, or is restricted to limited parts of the survey area. Interpretation of place-names is particularly helpful as it seems to hint at much greater antiquity of some sites or estate centres than we might expect from the other written sources. It points us towards important early sites that we should be looking for. In the meantime we have to rely on instinct, based on research and common sense, to interpret what has happened around Montrose Basin in the past and to extrapolate the findings in local and national terms.

Unexpected Sites

In all the periods studied during the survey, despite the ebb and flow of history, there appear examples of the unusual or exceptional. Perhaps five-and-a-half-thousand years ago, an important centre for ritual started developing at the west end of the Basin. Dating from more than a thousand years later, one element of this complex – a converted Bronze Age barrow at Fordhouse of Dun – has yielded an exceptional series of burial goods. In the first century AD a Roman naval camp was established on the north side of the Basin – it is the only site of its type from this important campaign to conquer northern Scotland. The Pictish evidence is dispersed, but not only was there an early chapel site on Rossie Island as evidenced by the decorated stones found there, but more early sites should be expected from place-name evidence.

By the medieval period we have the planned Royal Burgh and castle, with Montrose climbing to become one of the more important towns in Scotland by the fourteenth century. The dense cluster of castle sites around the Basin is also extremely unusual. In the later-medieval period Montrose had an important school that held one of the finest libraries in Scotland. This may be the reason that by the sixteenth century, the Montrose area started producing some of the leading figures in the dialogues for religious reform, including Melville and later, Erskine of Dun. In the seventeenth century the Marquis of Montrose was one of the greatest military leaders in Britain, first for the Covenanters and then for the king.

By the eighteenth century substantial numbers of local residents were involved in the West Indian trade. They brought huge sums of money back into the area, allowing the redevelopment of the major houses and estates of the Montrose Basin area in the 'enlightened' style. At the same time, in the wider world, men from the town were at the forefront of the development of the Empire. In the nineteenth century (as industry was developing in the town) external interest had been largely transferred from the Americas to the East and locals had key roles in the East India Company, Army or Navy. To name but two residents of the town, Alexander Burnes had been involved in exploits across the Middle East, before dying in the Kabul rising of 1841. Robert Brown, more peacefully, started his career as a naturalist on the Australian expedition of the HMS *Investigator* between 1801 and 1805, before becoming the secretary and literary heir to Sir Joseph Banks, the leading naturalist of his time.

By the middle of the nineteenth century the town was falling into relative decline, its harbour too small to compete with other major Scottish ports. Its industry too was by this time of only regional importance, in spite of the large mill complex, Paton's Works. Nevertheless, in the latter part of the nineteenth century and the 20th, the area saw a cultural flourish with a number of writers – Violet Jacob, Willa Muir, Fionn Maccolla and Hugh McDiarmaid – born or located here. William Lamb, the sculptor, had his studio in the town and many of his finest sculptures are still located there, although the paintings of Edward Baird are now considered so important that they are scattered more widely. What will the twenty-first-century cycle bring?

Time Line

The Time Line aims to give a chronological context to the history of the Montrose Basin area. The Line is divided into three columns: the first, giving dates; the second, local events corresponding to the date. The final column places these within a wider context, latterly defining this by naming the current monarch and major historical events including important battles.

Each page of Time Line is accompanied by a page of text placing the events in a broader political and social context.

Archaeological evidence consists of finds, either chance or from excavations, and, more recently, sites that have been identified by aerial photography of crop marks. The way crops grow, when seen from the air, shows ditches and walls: ditches where crops grow higher and ripen less quickly and walls where crops grow slower and ripen faster. Both finds and sites are placed at the time of their origin in the Time Line.

Symbols: ▲ = Find   ⊕ = Site   ⚔ = Battle

Million years ago		
4400	Pre Cambrian Era	The Earth forms
545	Paleozoic Era – Cambrian Period	Oldest multi-celled animals
495	Ordovician Period – Wide ocean between North America (inc Scotland) and Europe (inc England & Wales)	
440	Silurian Period	Mountains begin to form Ocean gradually closes
417	Devonian Period – Old Red Sandstone is the earliest geology of the Montrose area. Rivers and Volcanoes form the landscape	
354	Carboniferous Period	Tropical conditions, reptiles appear
250	Mesozoic Era – Triassic Period	North Sea and the Minch form. Dinosaurs & mammals appear
142	Cretaceous Period	Dinosaurs disappear. Flowering plants appear
65· 5	Cenozoic Era – Palaeocene Period	Atlantic Ocean forms
1· 81	Quaternary Period – Pleistocene Epoch. Periodic glaciations alternating with more temperate weather. Each glacial episode removed evidence of the previous one. The coastal lands rise and fall with the climate changes altering the coastline continuously throughout the Ice Age	
0· 01 or 10,000 years ago or 8000	Holocene Epoch	Post-glacial to present

Geology

Geologists measure time in millions of years, an unfathomable concept for the mind. To appreciate the time-scale of the formation of Montrose Basin requires us to comprehend vast aeons of time. The time line is shown on a sliding scale, greatly compressed in the distant past. The Geological Time Scale is divided into four eras: **Precambrian** (formation of the earth) **Paleozoic** (ancient life), **Mesozoic** (middle life) and **Cenozoic** (new life). These eras are subdivided into periods, mostly named after locations exemplifying a period's geology; Cambrian, for example, comes from the Latin word for Wales, the location of the world's earliest known fossils. Others, such as Carboniferous (coal bearing), are more descriptive. The Cenozoic periods are further divided into epochs.

An area may have an entirely different geology than that of its geographical neighbour, insomuch that continents have drifted apart or collided and seas opened and disappeared over the millennia. In the Ordovician Period, 495 million years ago, there was a wide ocean between the landmass that would eventually become North America, which in that Period included Scotland, and the landmass which is now Europe and which then included England and Wales. Over many millennia this ocean gradually closed, continents drifted and new oceans were created. Geological evidence is preserved in the rocks, and in studying these, a clear idea of the ancient geography can be found.

There are two periods of great significance in the geological make-up of the lands surrounding Montrose Basin. The oldest of these dates to the Devonian Period, 417–354 million years ago, when the Old Red Sandstone Continent was formed. Although covered by this generic name a great variety of rock types occur, including conglomerates, shales and limestone as well as sandstones. Volcanic activity was also common producing igneous rock as can be seen at Scurdie Ness. Fast flowing rivers emerging from mountain corries produced sediment as they reached flatter ground and from these areas there is fossil evidence of primitive fish, arthropods and plantlife.

There is a gap of many millennia before evidence of the other major geological episode, when 1,810,000 years ago a worldwide deterioration in climate occurred and great ice sheets covered the land. Glacial episodes were interspersed with more temperate conditions when the ice melted. Each new glacial period removed evidence of the previous episode. Sea levels were low during glaciation, but the land was also depressed under the weight of the ice; as the ice melted, flooding the land, the land slowly rose, but sea levels also rose. The changing levels of both the land and the sea resulted in fluctuation between dry land and shallow seas in coastal regions. As the land started to rise after the final glacier melted and the weight of the ice was removed, staircases of raised beaches formed along the East Coast producing cliffs like those seen at St Cyrus.

After the last glacier receded, it left a wide bay from Scurdie Ness to St Cyrus, which reached as far inland as Farnell, into which flowed the rivers North and South Esk.

Pre 8000BC	Palaeolithic Stone Age	
8000BC	Mesolithic Stone Age – People were nomadic Hunter/gatherer/fishers	
5000BC	Tsunami – Huge tidal wave caused by a landslide off the coast of Norway hits the east coast of Scotland	
	Gradually shingle accumulated in the wide estuary into which the rivers North and South Esk flow. A series of spits build up eventually closing off the bay on the north side. This shingle bank is divided into two halves: the inland half where mud and silt were deposited and the sea half where blown sand built up the Links. This bank eventually defines Montrose Basin as we see it today.	
3500BC	Neolithic Stone Age – People began to adopt agriculture and became more settled. Large communal monuments were built	
	⊕ Cursus (linear monument) from Powis to Old Montrose	First of series of Egyptian Pharaoh dynasties c3100BC
	⊕ Remains of timber structure and ditches under Fordhouse of Dun Barrow	Skara Brae c3000BC
	⚠ Scrapers from Old Montrose, Maryton, Bonnyton and Hillside	First Pyramids builtc2650BC
	⚠ Axes from Scurdie Ness, Hillside, Bridge of Dun and Montrose Basin	
2500BC		Stonehenge c2500BC

Stone Age

The Stone Age is divided into periods: **Palaeolithic** (ancient Stone Age) pre 8,000BC, **Mesolithic** (middle Stone Age) 8,000–3,500BC and **Neolithic** (new Stone Age) 3,500–2,500BC. As soon as the glaciers receded and the ice melted plants started to colonise the land and animals came, probably closely followed by the first people, Mesolithic man. These hunter/gatherer/fishers fashioned tools of flint and stone and built traps for fish. Because of their nomadic existence no monuments remain and we can only recognise their presence by archaeological finds.

Around 7,000 years ago (c5,000BC) a great tidal wave or *tsunami* hit the East Coast of Scotland, caused by a huge rock slide off the coast of Norway. Evidence for this is found in a thin layer of sand, rich in sea-life fossils, which can be found as far inland as Farnell. This natural disaster would have had a catastrophic effect on any human communities of the Mesolithic period living in the area.

Gradually shingle banks built up along the mouth of the bay between the two rivers, eventually closing off the north side of the bay. This bank is divided into two halves; clay deposits forming on the inland side and sand dunes on the seaward side. The area to the west of this spit of land becomes Montrose Basin and remains tidal.

The Neolithic Age is marked by a distinct range of archaeological sites as people adopted agriculture, these skills having originated in Eastern Europe and Asia thousands of years earlier. Whether brought to Scotland by mass immigration or a more gradual process of adoption, farming was established on the rich carselands round the Basin. These early farmers felled trees to clear the land for agriculture, using the wood for tool handles, fencing and building. They had domestic animals such as sheep, goats and cattle. Grinding stones show they grew cereals for flour, cloth was spun from flax, and they made simple pottery. All this evidence points to settled communities which, no doubt, still hunted from the rich fauna and fishing but had a more rooted existence than their Mesolithic forebears. The seaways would have been the easiest and most probable routes of travel, and since there is some evidence of trade, these people must have had seafaring skills.

Knowledge of these people and their religion, rituals and customs is based on finds and interpretations of burial and ceremonial structures, usually called long barrows, which have been identified or excavated. Another monument is a cursus (so named because eighteenth-century archaeologists thought the shape resembled a racecourse, *cursus* in Latin) an example of which can be seen southwest of the Basin at Powis. This is a long avenue defined by ditches whose function and importance to the people living round it can only be speculated over. Stone Age monuments were often reused by later peoples and the cursus has a circular enclosure at one end, which is probably Iron Age. Beneath the Bronze Age barrow at Fordhouse the wooden remains of a Neolithic structure were also found.

2500BC	**Bronze Age**

⊕ Maryton Law Barrow (excavated – finds include sherds of pottery, flint tools and large, clear crystal)

⊕ Fordhouse of Dun Barrow (excavated – finds include 38 separate ceramic pots and accompanying cremations)

⊕ Ring ditches (possibly Bronze Age) at Dun, Dubton & Old Montrose

Rise of the Greek civilisation *c*1200BC

⚔ Barbed and tanged arrowhead find at Newmanswalls

⚔ Looped Palstave (type of axe head) find at Rossie Island

⚔ Gold jewellery find north of Montrose town

Standing Stone Field (situated north of Montrose Town and referred to in Town records until 17th century) possibly dates from the Bronze Age

c800BC ⚔ Bronze Sword find at Montrose

800BC onwards **Iron Age**

Defences – Dun and Dunninald placenames indicate forts

Roman Republic 510BC

⊕ Promontory Fort at Scurdiness

⊕ Enclosure at end of Cursus at Powis

⚔ Iron Sword find at Balwyllo

Roman Empire 27BC

AD81 ⊕ Roman Naval Camp on north side of Basin near Gilrivie

⚔ Mons Graupius AD84

⚔ Stone oil lamps finds at Dun

⚔ Gold ring and Roman Intaglio (engraved insert for ring) finds, both at Usan

Bronze and Iron Ages

The introduction of metal for tools and decoration happened around 2,500BC. Bronze is made by smelting copper ore and adding tin which results in a bright, hard, durable metal. Copper ores are readily available in Angus but tin is much rarer and the closest supplies would have been Devon, Cornwall or Europe. The peoples who brought this new technology are generally known as the Beaker People because of the characteristic shape of their pottery. They may have been an invading culture or traders or a combination of the two, but their impact was permanent.

Burial and ritual practices seem to change around this time and the use of round barrows becomes widespread; two of which have been excavated at Fordhouse of Dun and Maryton Law. Life would have continued much as in the Stone Age with farming and fishing. A very early method of catching fish in rivers is a *cruive* – a dyke built out from both banks of a river with a gap in the middle into which wicker traps were built – and these may well date from this period.

The later stages of the Bronze Age appear more unsettled with an increase in the amount of weaponry and the establishment of enclosed settlements, some of which eventually become fortified.

The term Iron Age (from *c*800BC) is descriptive of a period which brought knowledge of a new skill and a subtle transition from the use of bronze to iron, made by smelting iron ores to produce a harder, more durable metal. Ditched enclosures which are defended homesteads, again identified by aerial photography, are scattered round the Basin and it is likely that many of these are Iron Age. Place-names with the *Dun* element, like Dun itself and Dunninald, point to fort sites. Defended hill fort settlements, like those at the Cathertuns, further inland in Angus, which had ditches, walls and gateways to restrict access, also suggest a society of tribal chiefdoms. This is the period where further north in Scotland brochs were built for defensive purposes and so it seems a more warlike culture was emerging.

Unlike further south the area was not settled by the Romans. However, there were raids and a Roman naval supply camp was established on the north side of the Basin, close to Gilrivie Farm. Agricola's campaign with the defeat of the native population at Mons Graupius in AD84 was followed by Roman retreat. Hadrian's Wall from the Tyne to the Solway was built in AD122, followed by the Antonine Wall, along the Forth Clyde valley in AD141. Septimus Severus marched north as far as Stonehaven in his AD208–212 campaigns, and archaeological finds reveal some Roman presence.

Date	Events	Wider Scotland
*c*100	⊕ Square barrows at Old Montrose	St Ninian arrives in Scotland *c*400
*c*500	St Brioc – the church at Inchbrayock, situated on Rossie Island was dedicated to St Brioc (also spelled Bruic or Broc)	
*c*570	St Skae – the ruined chapel dedicated to St Skae (also known as St Skaoch) lies on the clifftop near Boddin Point. She came from Ireland, perhaps with St Columba. The old parish of Dunninald was known as St Skaochy prior to the Reformation	St Columba arrives in Scotland 563
		✕ Dunnichen (Nechtansmere) 685
*c*750	St Fergus – the chapel dedicated to St Fergus lies near Mains of Usan farm. He was a Pict who trained for the priesthood in Ireland. He died at Glamis *c*750	
		Kings of Scots: Kenneth MacAlpin ?842–858
*c*850–950	⚔ The sculptured stones of Inchbrayoch (now held in Montrose Museum) and Farnell (now held in Pictavia) date from this period	
*c*850 onwards	Pictish language was giving way to Gaelic	Donald I 858–862 Constantine I 862–876
*c*900	⚔ Viking grave pin find from Fordhouse of Dun	Donald II 899–900 Constantine II 900–943 Malcolm I 943–954
		Kenneth II 971–995
	Norse influence *Stromnay* (meaning tidal-race island) a place-name used up to 14th Century also *Gait* (meaning street) as in Seagait	Kenneth III 997–1005

Picts and Scots

The Picts are an enigmatic race. They left virtually no written information, but their lives can be glimpsed by their artistic achievements, in particular their carved stones. These show hunting scenes, animals, heavily decorated crosses and mysterious symbols, and also one of their preoccupations – warfare. Descended from the Iron Age tribes, they encompassed early waves of Celtic invaders arriving in northeast Scotland. It is likely that they spoke a Celtic language, akin to Cornish and Welsh, elements of which survive in place-names, typically *Pit*, *Aber* and *Pert*. Their society had an aristocratic element with kingships and a complicated system of control by inter-marriage and extended families. They first appeared under the name Picts in Roman times; *Picti* is Latin for 'painted ones'. The Picts resisted the Roman advances very effectively and conducted three wars against them between AD380 and 460.

In Pictish times the area round the Basin remained densely populated because of the rich farmlands and fishing. Burial practices changed and square barrows covered interments. Their religion before the advent of Christianity can only be guessed at and when the first Christian missionaries arrived they appropriated as many of the pagan customs and sites as they could. Some ancient sites were dedicated to St Mary including Maryton (St Mary's of Old Montrose). Numbers of monks came over from Ireland, the birthplace of the Culdee Church, and remains of chapels dedicated to early saints can be seen locally in typically isolated cliff top sites, such as the chapels of St Skae and St Fergus. Fine carved stones were placed at Inchbrayock (Rossie Island) and Farnell bearing both crosses and Pictish symbols.

Picts fought Britons, Scots and Northumbrians over territory in Scotland. The latter's expansion in the east was halted by Bridei, King of Picts, at the battle of Dunnichen (Nechtansmere) near Forfar in AD685. The Irish Annals refer to 'the might of the Pictish fleet' and the communities living round the Basin no doubt had substantial maritime skills. There were battles with the Vikings and most importantly with the Scots, with whom the Picts eventually merged in AD843 under the rule of Kenneth MacAlpin (part Pict himself). Thereafter the Picts gradually fade from history and by the tenth century were assimilated with the Scots.

The Scots emigrated from Ulster about AD500 and established the Kingdom of Dalriada in southwest Scotland. They were Gaelic speakers and as they gradually emerged as the more powerful race their language also spread. Typical place-name elements include *Bal*, *Kin* and *Craig*.

Early historians recorded several major Scandinavian invasions including the early sacking of Montrose, however, there is only limited evidence of Viking influence. *Stromnay*, Norse for tide-race island, is the name used for the port of Montrose in charters up to 1494. A Viking pin, found during the excavation of the barrow at Fordhouse of Dun possibly shows Scandinavian re-use of a previous culture's burial site.

*c*1000	Mormaers were members of the ancient Celtic aristocracy and the king's representatives in their district. They were the local overlords and dispensed justice, levied the taxes due to the king and organised military service. ' Mormaer'gave way to the term ' Earl'by the late-12th century.	Malcolm II 1005 Duncan I 1034 Macbeth 1040 Lulach 1058 Malcolm III 1058 (Canmore) ⚔ Hastings 1066
	Thanes were managers of the land for overlords, but on a smaller scale than the mormaers. Thanes appear in the records in Scotland at the beginning of the 10th century in the reign of Malcolm II (1005-34). There were Thanes locally at Old Montrose, Kinnaber, Morphie, Ecclesgreig and Inverkeilor.	Malcolm m. Margaret 1070 Donald Ban 1093 Duncan II Donald Ban 1093 Edgar 1097 Alexander I 1107 David I 1124
*c*1130	Royal Burgh of Montrose established	
*c*1165 1165	Castle at Montrose Lands of Dun granted to John of Hastings. First reference to Hedderwick	Malcolm IV 1153 William I 1165 (The Lion)
1178	Arbroath Abbey founded. Ferry rights over South Esk transferred to Arbroath Abbey. Annanie or Inyaney Estate (which included parts of Fullerton, Old Montrose & Bonnyton) was gifted to Crane – gatekeeper of castle of Montrose	Alexander II 1214
1244 1245	Fire destroys large part of Montrose Rossy: Hugh de Malherbe sold estate and castle to a vassal thereafter called de Rossy. De Malherbe also donated part of his lands to the hospital	Alexander III 1249 Queen Margaret canonised 1250
1261	Annanie left to five daughters and divided among them	
1270	Montrose one of the four principal ports of Scotland	

Scots and Normans

As Scotland emerged from the Dark Ages its borders were still largely undefined. The west and north was under Viking control. The border with England remained the focus of land disputes, battles and raids for centuries. Rival claims to kingship meant that more than a few kings met violent deaths, while alliances, cemented by marriage, between ruling families, often confused matters further. For example, Malcolm Canmore defeated Macbeth with a Northumbrian army. His first bride was Ingibjorg, widow of Thorfinn, Earl of Orkney, and his second, Margaret, an English Saxon princess, who was a refugee following the Norman Conquest of England. Queen Margaret, who was later canonised, instigated the reform of the church in Scotland, encouraging new Abbeys, a practice that was carried out by her sons and grandsons. As more monasteries prospered, clerics trained in Latin begin writing records, especially of the landed families providing a new historical source.

The influx of a new nobility began with the accession of King David in 1124, who had spent many years at the English court. Many Norman lords were invited north and given lands, driving out the Celtic aristocracy and introducing the feudal system. Baronies were created: an estate was granted to knights or important members of the king's household, in return for their fealty and service. These nobles, in their turn, let out holdings and demanded men to fight for them and the king. Sheriffs were appointed and lived in the royal residence. They were responsible for administering the law and raising taxes. Ownership by Scottish royalty of lands in England meant English kings expected fealty and military support, not always forthcoming, producing further tension between the nations.

The seaways remained important and King David founded several Royal Burghs, to channel trade and thus gather customs. Montrose, then known as Sallork, was established as a Royal Burgh circa 1130. Controlled by burgesses, major tenants who controlled the town markets, Montrose rapidly became one of the wealthiest ports in Scotland. It had shipping links with the Baltic, Low Countries, France and Southern Europe and exported salmon, hides, wool and grain, while timber, wine and other luxuries were imported. Wealthy merchants, some Flemish, introduced new influences and societies of craftsmen began to flourish in the town. Scots, a version of Northern English spoken in the Lothians, spread by ripple effect as traders took advantage of the new trading opportunities, but it took many centuries to oust Gaelic. Typical elements include *burgh, den, -ton,* and *fauld.*

Normanisation of Angus began in the reign of William I. The effect on the language was minimal but many surnames including *Lindsay, Carnegie* and *Cummings* are all Norman in origin. Norman barons built castles to reflect their status. The affluence of the Basin area can be seen in the number of feudal estates that it supported around it: Usan, Craig, Rossie, Old Montrose, Annanie, Fullerton, Bonnyton, Dun, Ecclesjohn, Tayock, Hedderwick, Borrowfield and Newmanswalls.

Year	Event	Monarch
		Margaret 1286
		Interregnum 1290
		John Balliol 1292
1296	John Balliol stripped of kingship, while Edward I stays at Montrose Castle	Interregnum 1296
1297	Montrose Castle razed by William Wallace	
1300	Montrose has hospital	Robert I 1306 (Robert the Bruce)
		⚔ Bannockburn 1314
		Declaration of Arbroath
1325	Grahams acquire Old Montrose from Robert the Bruce	1320
1327	Lands of Fullerton with the office of King's Falconer granted to Geoffrey thereafter known as ' de Fullerton'	
1328	Maryton gifted to Walter Schaklok. Henry De Rossy buys part of Annanie from Walter Schaklok	
1329	School in Montrose	David II 1329
1349	' The Black Death' . Plague kills a third of population	
1369	Royal Charter gives fishings on North and South Esks to Montrose	
		Robert II 1371
1375	Sir Robert Erskine acquires Barony of Dun. Ecclesjohn Estate also acquired	
1377	John Erskine (grandson of Robert) first to be designated Laird of Dun	
		Robert III 1390
1393	William Tulloch received Bonnyton Castle	
		James I 1406
1409	Erskine of Dun mortifies (grants in perpetuity to an ecclesiastical estate) lands of Ecclesjohn to the Bishop of Brechin. Chapel at Ecclesjohn used by pilgrims	
1437	Sir Thomas Maule claims Lordship of Hedderwick	James II 1437
1446	Fullerton absorbed into Old Montrose	
1451	Barony of Old Montrose created	
		James III 1460
1484	David Rossy sold Usan to Walter Lichtoun	James IV 1488
1490	Erskines of Dun acquire Hedderwick	
1493	Dispute between townspeople of Montrose and Erskine of Dun over right to gather bait on Basin	
1498	Janet Tulloch sold her part of the mill at Bonnyton	

Late Medieval

Hostilities with the Vikings over the Western Isles ended, once again with marriage between the royal families, and Margaret, Maid of Norway inherited the Throne of Scotland. She was betrothed to Edward I of England's son and expected to rule an independent kingdom, but died on her journey south to Scotland. Many Scottish nobles claimed the throne and Edward I was asked to choose. He declared John Baliol king but demanded homage. France and Scotland pledged to come to each other's aid if invaded by England, an agreement thereafter known as the 'Auld Alliance'. Edward I retaliated by invading Scotland. He stayed in Montrose Castle while Baliol was stripped of his kingship. English garrisons occupied the castles and England controlled the country's affairs. Edward I forced an oath of loyalty from almost all Scottish noblemen in a document called the Ragman Roll.

Although the Wars of Independence begin with small bands of rebels, including those led by Wallace, resistance grew to include some leading Scots families. Robert the Bruce had himself crowned King of Scots and, by means both fair and foul, united the Scottish lords and led them to victory at the Battle of Bannockburn against Edward II. The Declaration of Arbroath 1320 was a plea for the Scottish nation to be recognised by the Pope. Victories and defeats for both sides continued. Raids and sieges were interspersed by periods of truce. Of the eight kings succeeding Bruce, only two were adults, so the country was frequently ruled by regents. Intrigue, murder and betrayal were endemic as the leading players jostled for power. By the turn of the fifteenth century neither the Scots nor the English could claim victory, but a coherent Scottish nation had emerged.

The royal estates round the Basin may have changed hands depending on the support of the incumbents, however, rural life continued much as ever and supported a large proportion of the population. The large estates would have rented out lands. Farmers and their cotters lived in *touns* of ten or so heather thatched cottages built of logs, rubble and turf. Rough barley and oat crops were grown in unenclosed fields and livestock including sheep, pigs and cattle were raised. Wool was spun and woven domestically. The estates would have tried to be self-sufficient and had mills, wind or water, fisheries and fishpools, woodland, dovecotes, warrens and gardens. Salt was essential for food preservation and was therefore a valuable commodity and a number of salt pans run by major baronies, including Arbroath Abbey, were sited round the Basin. Old Montrose had its own harbour where goods were landed within easier reach of Forfar and Brechin. Customs were collected there until the fifteenth century.

By the end of the fourteenth century the landed families availed themselves of both town and country houses allowing cosmopolitan and country living. However, when episodes of disease struck, such as the Black Death (bubonic plague) in 1349, anywhere where people lived in close proximity, almost everywhere, town or toun, the plague claimed about a third of lives – more than any war.

1500	House at Dun described as a tower house	
1505	3rd Lord Graham created 1st Earl of Montrose. David Rossy sold Craig to Andrew Wood of Largo	
1511	Barony of Usan created	
1513	1st Earl of Montrose slain at Flodden and four Erskines of Dun killed	Flodden 1513 James V 1513
1525	Salmon trade booming, although trade in Montrose had generally declined	Patrick Hamilton burnt 1528
1534	David Stratoun of St Cyrus burnt at the stake	
1540	John Erskine 5th Laird of Dun became Provost of Montrose	Mary I 1542 (Queen of Scots)
1541	John Erskine 5th Laird of Dun became Constable of Montrose	George Wishart burnt March 1546. Cardinal Beaton murdered May 1546
1548	English attempt to invade Montrose repelled at Battle of the Links. Fort built on site of present Infirmary	Rough Wooing 1547
1555/6	John Knox preaches at Dun Church occasionally in these years	
1556	John Lichtoun received lands of Usan including fishing and fishertown	
1557	John of Dun recognised as feuar of lands of Ecclesjohn by the Bishop of Brechin	
1558	Walter Miln, 80-year-old priest from Lunan, burnt as heretic	Reformation Parliament & first Assembly of Church of Scotland 1560 Mary Queen of Scots returns to Scotland 1561
1565	Sir John Erskine Moderator of General Assembly	
1567	Fishing rights on North Esk transferred from Friars of St Mary's at Montrose to Wishart of Pitarrow	Mary abdicated 1567 James VI 1567
1574	Andrew Melville of Baldovie returns to Scotland and becomes leading academic spokesman for the Kirk for next 30 years	
1583	Benefices (parishes) of Ecclesjohn and Dun are united	'Black Acts' 1584 enforce King's rule over church
1590	Hedderwick passes to the Grahams	Mary Queen of Scots executed 1587
1599	3rd Earl of Montrose became Chancellor of Scotland	

Sixteenth Century

With the marriage in 1503 of James IV to Margaret Tudor, daughter of Henry VII of England, came several years of relative peace and prosperity for Scotland. Despite a general European recession the salmon trade continued to prosper and craft guilds were established. Three Scottish universities had been founded and the Education Act ensured that the elder sons of wealthy families had learning in Latin and law. Selling feus had became a common source of income for the Crown and the Church. The first printing press in Scotland was set up in 1507 and printed Acts of Parliament, prayer books and even poetry, but this golden age of the Scottish Renaissance did not last long. Henry VIII succeeded to the English throne in 1509 and invaded France in 1513. The 'Auld Alliance' was again resurrected. James IV marched his army south with disastrous consequences – 10,000 Scots died at the Battle of Flodden, men of all rank including the king. The heir was a child so, once more, regents ruled until James V reached adulthood

James V took two French brides, but died when his heiress, Mary was only days old. Henry VIII, who had declared himself head of the Church of England in 1534, wanted Mary to marry his son, and so began a series of attacks on Scotland, known as the 'rough wooing'. The young queen was sent to France for safety and by the time she returned, widowed and childless, in 1561, she was a Catholic queen of a largely Protestant country.

The Protestant movement, which originated in Germany, had gradually spread through Europe. In Scotland, bishoprics and other lucrative clerical positions had been allocated to those in the service of the crown, while the parish priests were left to struggle with little money and education. Montrose and district was one of the strongholds of Reform. Given the town's importance as a seaport it is likely that 'heretical' copies of the Bible, translations in languages other than Latin, were imported through Montrose from the early 1530s. This, along with the presence of some of the leading players, may have been partly responsible for the reforming zeal that spread throughout the area. The Scottish Reformation occurred thirty years later than in England and therefore had more Calvinistic ideals. However, not enough Protestant ministers were available and many churches were left with 'readers', often the former Catholic priests. The spread and development of the 'new' religion was not consistent.

Mary was forced to abdicate in 1567. Once again Scotland was left with a child king and nobility fighting over regency and power. The merchants continued to control the towns, although the power of the craft guilds had increased. In 1563 witchcraft was made a crime. Several years of bad weather and famine contributed to the growing gap between rich and poor. The numbers of beggars, peddlers and the destitute grew. By the time James VI took control of the country Scotland was poverty-stricken and disorderly. This king, however, was also heir to another richer throne.

Year	Event	National Context
		Union of Crowns 1603 James VI of Scotland becomes James I of England
1612	10th Laird of Dun, a boy called John, poisoned by his Uncle Robert and his sisters. James Graham born (becomes 1st Marquis of Montrose)	
1615	Craig owned by Carnegies. George Erskine of Kirkbuddo inherits Ecclesjohn	
1618	Parishes of Dunninald and Craig united	
1626	4th Earl of Montrose is President of the Council of Scotland	Charles I 1625
1630	Erskines of Kirkbuddo acquire Hedderwick	
1641	Old Montrose ransacked by Covenanters. Repaired 1642	National Covenant 1638 Solemn League and Covenant 1643
1644	James Graham plunders Dun after Montrose citizens – pro-Covenanters – hid their valuables there as the town had already been raided by Irvine of Drum. James Graham created 1st Marquis of Montrose and Lt General of Scotland	
1648/9	Plague in Montrose killing half the population. Harbour closed, Town Council meetings suspended. Plague pits for dead sited on Links	Charles I executed in 1649. Charles II (in exile) proclaimed King in Edinbugh
1650	Marquis of Montrose executed in Edinburgh	Scotland formally unified with England and Ireland under Cromwell in 1653 – Commonwealth
1659	Patrick Scott acquires Craig. James Scott buys Hedderwick. New house built	Charles II 1660 Restored
1663	Patrick Scott buys Rossie Estate	
1666	Barony of Bonniton created	
1668	Old Montrose Barony given to John, Earl of Middleton	
1670	Dun sells Land of Sands to Robert Raitt for Dronner's Dyke	
1678	Dronner's Dyke built but destroyed within a year by storm reputedly conjured up by Montrose witch Maggie Cowie	James VII & II 1685 William II & III of Orange & Mary 1689 (Joint Sovereigns)
1690	Patrick Renny bought Usan	Massacre of Glencoe 1692
1690s	Five years of famine caused the death or dispersal of almost a third of rural population	Mary's death. Sole reign of William II & III 1694

Seventeenth Century

James VI succeeded to the English throne and removed his court south of the border. When his son Charles I tried to impose a new Service Book in Scotland in 1637 the Convention of Tables, made up of nobility, gentry, ministers and burgesses, which, opposed to the king as Head of the Church, drew up the National Covenant in 1638. Royalist and Covenanting armies met, but agreed an uneasy truce. The English Civil War and the Covenanting wars of Scotland ran concurrently and are intertwined and complex.

The Solemn League and Covenant was agreed in 1643, but James Graham, later first Marquis of Montrose, wary of extremism, refused to sign. The English parliamentary army paid Scottish Covenanters for their support. The Royalist campaigns of the Marquis of Montrose achieved considerable success up to 1645, until Charles I surrendered to the Covenanters and Montrose was exiled. Cromwell executed Charles I without consultation with the Scottish parliament. An exiled Charles II was declared king in Scotland. He sent Montrose to retake Scotland by force but also colluded with Argyll's Presbyterian government and Montrose was captured and executed. Charles II arrived back in Scotland, was 're-educated' by Covenanters and crowned at Scone. Cromwell invaded and won decisively – Charles II fled to France, leaving Scotland with no king, an English government and General Monck's army in occupation.

However, Cromwell's death in 1658 led to the Restoration of Charles II, ironically won with the aid of General Monck's army. The Privy Council was re-established to govern Scotland and bishops reinstated in the Church. Although covenanting resistance continued, Charles's brother and successor James VII & II, a Catholic, conceded religious toleration. He fled from England in 1688, during the 'Glorious Revolution', and the influence and power of royalty lessened from this period. The Scottish Parliament of Estates followed the English lead and also decreed in favour of William and Mary, in return for abolition of the episcopacy. Mary was James VII's daughter, but both were grandchildren of Charles I. There was support for James in Scotland, and led by John Graham of Claverhouse, now Viscount Dundee, they won the Battle of Killiecrankie in 1689. But the rebellion petered out after 'Bonnie Dundee' died in that battle.

Although the infamy of the 1680s 'Killing Times', when covenanters were hunted down, is remembered, the plague certainly claimed more lives. Witch hunts, also took an incredible toll: 300 witches were executed in the year 1660 alone in Scotland. Weaving, though still mainly a cottage industry, began to be organised into guilds in towns. Potatoes were introduced, but most of the cattle reared was exported on the hoof to England and the Scots diet was mainly grain-based. English controls over trade, including an embargo on Scottish trade with English colonies, limited the Scottish economy. The fiasco of the Darien project, whereby an attempt at starting a Scottish Colony failed drastically, virtually bankrupted the nation. The Massacre at Glencoe in 1692, initiated by the Scottish parliament, shocked the nation. Years of terrible harvests and famine increased poverty and led to further discontent.

1700s	Lime Kiln built at Hedderwick. Period of Milnes at Ecclesjohn. New mansion house built	Anne 1702 Act of Union 1707
1715	The Old Pretender (James VIII) spends his last night in Scotland as guest of Scott of Hedderwick	George I 1714 Jacobite Rising 1715
1726	Col Scott buys Ecclesjohn	George II 1727
1730	New house built at Dun designed by Adam	
1739	Glenskenno Spring acquired as water supply for Montrose	
1740	Hedderwick largely rebuilt	
1742	Scott of Rossie held all sixteen sixteenths of Montrose Town fishings	
1745	Naval Battle at Montrose. English sloop *The Hazard* captured by Jacobites. French ship *La Fine* sunk off Rossie Island	Jacobite Rising 1745
1746	Cumberland's army billeted at Montrose after Culloden	⚔ Culloden 1746 George III 1760 American Declaration of Independence 1776
1780	Duncans acquire Rosemount and build new house	
1781	Montrose Lunatic Asylum built on Links. First in Scotland	
1783	Hercules Ross buys Rossie and Craig estates	
1785	' Outside' firms, mostly from Berwick, begin to take over salmon tacks	
1786	Bridge of Dun erected	
1787	George Oglivy buys Ecclesjohn, changes its name to Langley Park	
1791	Carnegies of Kinnaird buy Old Montrose	French Revolution 1789
1793	James Cruikshank buys Langley Park	
1795	Wooden Bridge over South Esk erected. Annual horse racing begins on racecourse on Links	
1799	Inch Bridge erected	

Eighteenth Century

Once again relationships between Scotland and England deteriorated. Queen Anne, Mary's sister, was unable to produce a surviving heir despite having seventeen children. The English parliament chose the Hanoverian decendancy from James VI for succession, without referring to the Scottish parliament. Although there were serious objections in Scotland, the economy was crippled and the threat of further withdrawal of English trade and citizenship persuaded the Scots to accept the Act of Union. The 'Old Pretender', designated James VIII although never crowned, attempted to land in Fife in 1708 but was repelled. The subsequent Jacobite Rising of 1715 was poorly led and badly organised.

The last Jacobite Rising in 1745, led by Charles Stuart, James VIII's son, on his father's behalf, was initially more successful. With support of the Highland Chiefs, the Episcopalians and those resentful of the Union, the young Prince marched his army as far South as Derby, before retreating back to the Highlands. Defeat at Culloden ended the Stuart cause. The killing and retribution, however, continued throughout Scotland. The Duke of Cumberland's troops were quartered inside Montrose but, despite the town's Jacobite sympathies, were persuaded not to sack it.

Although the 1560 Reformation ideal of establishing parish schools did not have an immediate effect, by the mid-eighteenth century Scotland did have an education structure available to all classes, if male. For Scots the best opportunities for wealth lay abroad in the expanding British Empire and many went to work for the East India Company or west to the colonies of America and the West Indies. They filled the demand for administrators, soldiers, lawyers and doctors. Trade with the West Indies, importing sugar and tobacco and linked with the transportation of slaves from Africa, brought considerable wealth to some families. In the latter part of the century the Scottish Enlightenment movement flourished producing renowned artists, poets and architects.

The economic and social transformation of Scotland accelerated. As the textile industry was transformed from cottage to factory-based production, employment in the towns increased. The formerly rural society dependent on subsistence agriculture became increasingly urbanised. Agricultural improvements were introduced to meet the demand for food from the growing towns. Major land improvements began including marsh and bog reclamation, field enclosure, crop rotation and liming, but improvements were sporadic, depending on the estate owner, although many estates round the Basin were at the forefront of the agricultural revolution. Banking and commercial infrastructure were developed; roads and internal transport improved. Locally, there was extensive building on estates, using 'new' money made abroad. Bridges were erected on the South Esk at Dun and Rossie Island. The whaling industry brought new business to the harbour and the ship building industry also grew. The abolition of the Coal tax, in 1793, allowed major heavy industrial developments round the port, including two new salt works and lime works. Continuous wars in Europe and the colonies increased the London government's need for manpower and, as confidence in the loyalty of the Scottish soldier grew, Scottish regiments became an established part of the British Armed Forces.

1800	First lifeboat at Montrose	
1805	Rossie Castle completed by Hercules Ross	
1809	Bothy system begins to be used in Angus farms	
1815	Glenskenno added to Langley Park estate	⚔ Waterloo 1815
1817	Draining of the Lurgies at west edge of Basin	
1818	South Esk leading lights first lit	
1820s	Whaling Industry reaches its peak	George IV 1820
1825	Joseph Johnston begins salmon company in Montrose	
1829	Suspension Bridge over South Esk opened	William IV 1830
1835	Royal Infirmary opens Windmill Hill, near the port area, removed	Abolition of Slavery 1833 Victoria 1837
1838	Gas Works built, gas light in town. Wet Dock building began, opened 1843	
1842	Montrose Museum built	
1845	Public Baths built just to west of Suspension Bridge near the Infirmary	Corn Laws repealed 1846
1853	Building began of the new Psychiatric Hospital at Sunnyside. Old buildings sold to War Office for barracks	Crimean War begins 1854 Indian Mutiny 1857
1865	Montrose–Bervie Railway opens	
1870	Scurdie Ness Lighthouse first lit (Stevenson)	Education Act 1872
1880	North British Railway South Esk viaduct opens	Tay Bridge Disaster 1879
1883	Montrose–Arbroath railway opened for passenger traffic	
1893	Rossie island bought by Town Council	
1895	First burial at Sleepyhillock Cemetery. Rossie Island transferred to Montrose Parish from Craig	Boer War begins 1899

Nineteenth Century

The revolution in France had sparked political debate throughout the country. France declared war in 1793 and threatened invasion. Some of the coast was fortified with Martello towers housing militia. The war lasted until 1815 and many young Scots were press-ganged into the navy, especially from those areas which had a maritime tradition.

In the Highlands there was mass migration of the population. Some was imposed by the Clearances, where land was cleared of people to make way for sheep, but severe poverty and famine also contributed. Many set out for the colonies, but huge numbers also moved into the towns and cities of central Scotland. Late-eighteenth and early-nineteenth centuries was the era of 'new' money. Locally the estates of Langley Park and Rossie flourished under rich owners with West Indian investments, while George Keith of Usan made a fortune in South Carolina and Rosemount was built with profits from the East India Company.

The whaling industry reached its peak in the 1820s and stimulated ship building growth. The salmon trade was also growing, with the introduction of stake nets at the turn of the century along with packing in ice, introduced by George Dempster of Dunnichen. The fish were sent south to London in small coastal smacks and later, with the introduction of the railways, by train.

Railways were probably the single most dramatic development of Queen Victoria's long reign: they encouraged economic growth, perishable goods could be transported long distances and the population became more mobile. The railway system demanded building a new infrastructure of tracks and stations as well as encouraging civil engineering on a huge scale to link these. In Montrose two stations were built: the Caledonian station near the docks and, on the eastern edge of the Basin, the station for the Montrose–Arbroath line necessitated the demolition of part of the High Street and the creation of Hume Street.

The textile industry, boosted by the demand for sailcloth during the Napoleonic Wars, continued its growth and a large amount of flax was imported from the Baltic. Urban employment grew as several mills were sited in Montrose. Paton's Mill, built on the Mid Links, was one of the largest. The town's population grew fourfold during the century, but the increase in population also increased disease. Sanitation was poor. Dirty water often led to outbreaks of cholera and typhus and overcrowding aided the spread of tuberculosis.

Wood was another principal import, Montrose becoming Scotland's second largest timber port. Although herring had always been fished it was during the later part of the century that east coast fishermen began to go after the huge shoals that moved round the coast, changing from lines of baited hooks to drift nets. Bigger steam-powered boats were built, and villages such as Ferryden and Usan thrived. Women gutted and packed the fish, so there was employment for the entire community.

1901	Lifeboat Station built	Edward VII 1901
1910	Rossie and Craig estate split up and sold	George V 1910
1911	Ferry motorised	
1913	Aviation base established Upper Dysart	
1914	Aerodrome established on Links at Broomfield	1st World War 1914–1918
1919	Housing scheme begun on Rossie Island	
1931	New Bridge over South Esk opens	
1935	Military Air Station re-established at Broomfield	Edward VIII 1936 Abdicated 1936
1940s	South Esk Ferry ceases	George VI 1936
1940	Edwin Scott Luke buys Langley Park. Let to Air Ministry	2nd World War 1939–1945
1947	Redfield Housing Scheme commenced	
1949	Reconstruction of Langley Park – Top floor removed	
1950	Broomfield closed as a Military Base	
1952	Glaxo comes to Montrose	Elizabeth II 1952
1954	Brechin Road Housing Scheme commenced	
_c_1955	Newmanswalls House demolished having been burnt pre-war	
1957	Rossie Castle razed. Housing begun at Panter Crescent, Borrowfield	
1972	Borrowfield Housing Scheme completed. Glaxo Laboratories £2· 5 million extension. North channel of South Esk (also known as the Inch Burn) infilled and the Inch Bridge covered for the P&O oil base	America lands man on Moon 1969
1980	House of Dun bequeathed to the National Trust	
1981	Montrose Basin declared local Nature Reserve. Wet dock infilled	
1984	Ruins of Hedderwick house levelled for safety	
1993	Aerodrome Museum opens at Broomfield	
1995	Basin Wildlife Centre opened by Scottish Wildlife Trust	New Scottish Parliament 1999

Twentieth Century

At the beginning of the century horses were used to work the land and considerable manpower was needed in farming. By the new millennium, gigantic combine harvesters operated by a single person could harvest a huge acreage. The same rapid progress has changed every walk of life in the twentieth century. The internal combustion engine revolutionised not only farming, but also transport and industry. Flight, man's dream of emulating birds, was realised and one of Britain's first military aerodromes was built at Broomfield in 1914. It was operational though both World Wars and the Basin was used as a bombing range.

The herring industry reached its peak about 1910 but global events intervened. World war dominates the first half of the century with thousands of young men killed in the trenches in Europe in the First World War. Those who returned were at risk from the flu epidemic, which swept the country in 1919. Women, who had filled male occupations during the war years, finally won the vote that year. After the Second World War many rural communities and hamlets disappeared completely. The large estates declined and the age of large country houses with numerous servants disappeared. Urban housing schemes, initiated in the 1920s, continued throughout the century, including schemes on Rossie Island, at Borrowfield and round the northeast corner of the Basin. Scientific and medical breakthroughs, including the discovery of penicillin, which became available after the war, promoted health, as did the creation of the National Health Service in 1948.

The textile industry, which had again undergone resurgence at the turn of the century, finally ended in the 1960s. Shipbuilding ceased but the port continued to prosper with potato and grain exports. Joseph Johnston & Sons' salmon fishing business grew with stations from Usan to north of St Cyrus. New food processing plants and a growing tourist industry, along with the arrival of Glaxo's pharmaceutical company, in the 1950s and North Sea oil in the 1970s helped the area prosper. The Inch Burn, the south channel of the South Esk, was infilled and the Inch Bridge covered over in 1972 for the P&O Oil base and Rossie Island was no longer surrounded by water. By the century's end these industries also were mostly in decline, although the area still remains a popular holiday destination. The Basin had always been an important centre for wading and migrating birds, as well as flora and fauna and as a result the Wildlife Centre was built to provide a focal point.

The technical innovations of the last century have changed most aspects of life: computers, mobile phones, and space travel were all unimaginable concepts a mere hundred years ago. The residents of the Basin area will, no doubt, face new and unimaginable changes in the future also. Twice daily the Basin fills and empties as the sea ebbs and flows and we have no knowledge of what tomorrow's tide will bring.

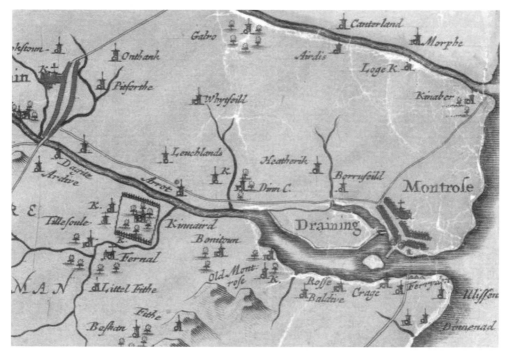

2 *Detail from* The Shire of Angus *(Rev Robert Edward, 1678) prematurely anticipating the reclamation of the Basin by Dronner's Dyke*

3 *Detail from* The Shire of Angus or Forfar *(Herman Moll, 1725)*

3   From Scurdie Ness to Dun Bridge

Place-names around Montrose Basin

About 7000 years ago, a pioneering tribe of hunter-gatherers wandered up the coast, perhaps in boats of hide and branches, perhaps searching for shellfish. Rounding Scurdie Ness, they first saw the area we now call Montrose Basin. It was then a wide estuary which reached almost as far inland as Brechin. These immigrants were the first of many, each group bringing with them their own language. These men and women would have needed to describe their surroundings, and in one sense, to name them. They did so not as a conscious process, but initially merely as a basic description of what they saw – without capital letters, so to speak.

Rivers, such as the South Esk, have from the earliest times played an important part in human affairs, as sources of drinking water, as means of travel, as obstacles to travel, and even as deities. It is perhaps not surprising, therefore, that the names of rivers have shown remarkable staying power. They are often the Methuselahs of the nomenclature of any district, and cannot be shown to belong to any later language. And in many cases, their names mean simply 'water', or describe some characteristic of the water. One such name is *Tay*, which may be incorporated in the local *Tayock Burn*. The name *Esk*, although not quite so venerable, also means water.

The language of these earliest arrivals can never be known. Apart from a few Bronze Age and Iron Age remains, the only traces of them may be the river names. Even the Romans, despite being the first literate incomers, left no impact on the place-names, either here or anywhere else in Scotland.

The Pictish Language

The first inhabitants of the area (as opposed to transient invaders such as the Romans) whose language can be identified, were the Picts. Their language was a branch of a Celtic group from which modern Welsh, Cornish and Breton also sprang. It was related to, but distinct from, the branch which has given us Scottish and Irish Gaelic.

The Picts have left us few written records other than King lists. They did not appear to be much interested in the effete business of writing, although there were scriptoria at monasteries such as Brechin, where the monks transcribed Latin texts. The energy channelled into writing in other cultures was, in the case of the Picts, used in the sculpting of the vigorous scenes on Pictish stones.

Angus was one of the main provinces of the Picts, and they did bequeath us some place-names to mark their sway. *Angus* itself, from *Oengus* or *Unguist* meaning 'unique choice', was originally a personal name but then applied to the area governed by a Mormaer, then to the Earldom, and finally to the County.

Pert, as in Logie Pert, meaning a wood or copse is another vestige of their language, as is *aber* (mouth or confluence of a river) which we find in *Kinnaber* (headland at the mouth of the river). This is an interesting name as it is a hybrid of Pictish and Gaelic elements, *kin-* or *ceann-* meaning 'at the head of' in Gaelic. Such hybrids are quite a common occurrence, perhaps indicating partial translation from an earlier form when Gaelic speakers were settling on Pictish lands.

Apart from *Pitarris Hill* and *Prettycur* (formerly *Pettycur*) the telltale Pictish form *pit-*, meaning a portion or share, appear to be largely absent from the area surrounding Montrose Basin, although it is interesting to note that on Ainslie's map of Angus of 1794, the farm we now know as *Balkeillie* is marked as *Pitkeilie*, the two prefixes having the same meaning. The coining of Pictish names began to fade with the coming of the MacAlpin dynasty in the late-ninth century, and the Pictish language was gradually superseded by Gaelic.

TRACES OF THE NORSEMEN

The Vikings also put their oar in. The Norsemen came frequently enough to give some places in the locality a name, such as *Stromnay* and possibly *Hedderwick*. They may have settled and 'intermarried' with the local inhabitants, who at that time were probably Pictish-speaking. There are a few other Norse place-names in Angus, such as *Grimsby* in Arbroath and *Ravensby* near Carnoustie, although more might have been expected considering their prevalence to the north and south.

However, some of those apparently Norse names such as *-ness* and *-haven* were borrowed earlier into northern England and came into eastern Scotland from the south rather than the east.

GAELIC AND SCOTS

A glance at the latest Ordnance Survey Map will show a large proportion of the names in the vicinity of Montrose Basin to be Gaelic or Scots in origin. Those with a Gaelic provenance range from *Montrose* itself and the *Annat Bank* in the east, to *Balwyllo* and *Balnillo* in the west. The fact that Gaelic and Scots names are so frequent in the area, and Pictish names less so, indicates that the take-over from Pictish-speaking peoples must have been fairly complete, and that many of the settlements must have been named, or renamed, in or after the ninth century.

The Gaelic language was gradually retreating behind the Highland Line and giving way to Scots in this area by the fourteenth or fifteenth century, initially in the burghs, like Montrose, which were colonised by Scots and Flemish speakers. The Scots language then spread gradually to the hinterland. But in the remoter areas such as the Angus Glens, Gaelic may have lingered on into the late-nineteenth century. The novelist Fionn MacColla, himself an offspring of Montrose, mentions a member of his parents' generation, born in the mid-nineteenth century in Glen Prosen, who 'either spoke Gaelic, or was familiar with the language in childhood'. On the other hand, David Dorward, writing as recently as 2001, can find no evidence for the survival of Gaelic in Glenesk beyond 1800.

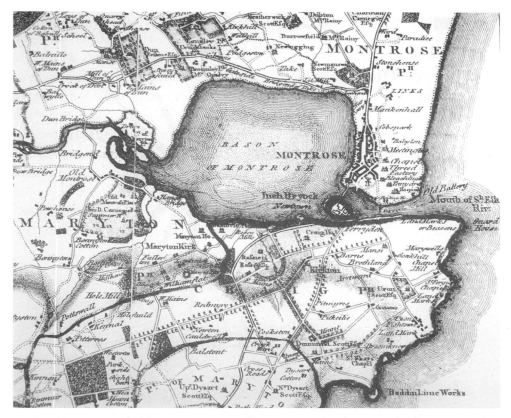

4 *Detail from* Map of the County of Forfar or Shire of Angus *(J Ainslie, 1794). (Caledonian Maps – www.caledonianmaps.co.uk)*

With the Union of the Parliaments in 1707, it became necessary for the gentry and the aristocracy to make themselves understood in London. Their outlandish Scots speech being largely unintelligible south of the Border, this was to prove something of a problem. On one occasion, three Lords of Justiciary were ordered to appear at the bar of the House of Lords in connection with the Porteous Riots. One of these was Lord Dun, 13th Laird of Dun, and builder of the present House of Dun, who pompously informed his two fellow judges –

> *Brethren, I am sorry to say that neither of you will be understood by the House tomorrow. I am, as you well know, in a different situation, having made the English language my particular study.*

As predicted, when tomorrow came, Lord Royston was hardly intelligible, but Lord Dun's pomposity was pricked when it was said of him, 'Deil ae word from beginning to end did the English understand of his speech'. From about the middle of the eighteenth century, this process of standardisation of speech spread through Scots society.

The Scots language has given us many of our local names, such as those ending in *-ton*, meaning farm. As a representative sample we have *Charleton* (farm of the carl, or churl, a serf), *Kirkton* (farm at the church), *Maryton* (farm at St Mary's Well), *Bonnyton* (bondman's farm), and *Fullerton* (fowler's farm). Scots speakers must also have named *Borrowfield* (field or open land belonging to the Burgh), *Newbigging* (new building), and *Broomley* (grass park with broom).

Although the Pictish names were, to a large extent, superseded by Gaelic ones from the ninth century, a bilingual period of transition resulted in some hybrid names. This was as a result of the gradual advance eastwards of the Gaelic-speaking people we now describe as Scots, culminating in the advent of Kenneth MacAlpin as King of Scots. What we know as the Scots language, however, was a later arrival, something of a johnny-come-lately in linguistic terms. This points up the curious anomaly that the word *Scots* is used on the one hand to describe a language originating as a variety of Northern English, and on the other, migrants who spread westwards from Dalriada, and amalgamated with the Picts to form the early Scottish kingdom. They did not speak Scots, however – they spoke Gaelic.

5 The Ebb Tide *by William Lamb. (From the collections of the William Lamb Studio)*

Sailing up the River

Perhaps the most interesting way to appreciate the place-names of the district would be to embark on a leisurely boat trip up the South Esk from Scurdie Ness to the Bridge of Dun, taking in the panorama of the low-lying hills of Angus, the scattered farms and the mud flats, with the grander elevation of the Grampians in the background.

The South Esk

Esk itself is a river name whose provenance is one of the oldest in the area, being one of the fairly large family of *Esk*, *Usk*, *Exe*, and *Axe*, no less than eleven of which in Britain were mentioned by the Romans. Five of these take the form *Esk*, and are all found north of Yorkshire. The word derives from a Continental Celtic word *isca* meaning 'water', or 'boggy place', which would fit well with the lower course and Basin of the South Esk.

The Gaelic *uisge*, which of course gives us the water of life — whisky, comes from the same source.

6 *Scurdie Ness Lighthouse. (Copyright: Alasdair Macdonald)*

Scurdie Ness

First, on our port side, is *Scurdie Ness* itself, the name meaning 'rocky point'. *Scurdie* is a Scots word for rock borrowed from the Gaelic *sgurr* meaning a peak or cliff. Several seventeenth- and eighteenth-century coastal charts show an outlying rock marked *sten* or stone, off Scurdie Ness which lends credence to it being a navigational name. A little south of the lighthouse can be seen the remains of a quarry. *Scurdie rock* quarried there was used for many buildings in Montrose, including much of the town walls, the old steeple and Dronner's Dyke, mentioned below.

Interestingly, in addition to referring to rocks in general, *scurdie* can mean 'a mooring stone', 'a resting place', either perhaps indicating shipping activity, or 'a favourite seat', a role which it has furnished for generations of Ferrydenners and Montrosians.

Johnnie Main's Harbour

Right in the shadow of the lighthouse, at the entrance to the river, a tiny creek is marked on old maps as *Johnny Main's Harbour* or *Creek of John Mayne*. This is said to have been the landing place of an eighteenth-century smuggler of that name who lived in a house on the west side of Rossie Island at the Trout Shot. Many tales were told of his exploits in avoiding the 'gaugers', those gentlemen whose job it was to preserve the income of the exciseman, and hence, the Exchequer.

Usan

The land on the south side of the river from Scurdie Ness almost to Ferryden is shown on old estate maps as belonging to the Usan Estate, owned at least from the fifteenth century by the Leighton or Lychton family.

The name *Usan* itself has gone through a tortuous series of changes, the earliest form being *Hulysham* in 1245. The Old English *-ham*, meaning village, is an unlikely derivation for this area so we may have to look elsewhere for a possible definition. This part of the east coast of Scotland is scattered with *-haven* names, meaning harbour, such as *Johnshaven*, *Miltonhaven* and *Stonehaven*. So we may have *Ulli's haven* or *Ulli's harbour* after a Norse settler of that name.

Another enterprising suggestion is that the name is a part translation of the Gaelic *port a chaolais* meaning harbour at the kyles or narrows, hence 'kyles-haven', which then became *Hulysham*. Later forms were *Howsane*, *Willishaven* and *Ullyshaven*. In a Charter of 1704 James Scott is described as being of *Ulysseshaven*, and this lofty tag is repeated in Montrose Burgh Records in 1711 and 1732. The principal memorial at St Mary's Chapel at Mains of Usan is for Patrick Renny de *Ulysseshaven*, who died in 1735. Although the ancient Greek hero was certainly well travelled, no evidence has yet been produced that his Odyssey took in East Angus! The name was later contracted to *Usan*.

Annat Bank

Depending on the state of the tide, on our starboard side we can now see a portion of the Annat Bank, long a hazard to navigation, particularly in the days of sail.

The name *Annat* goes back a long way, being marked on Adair's map of 1693 and on Captain Greenville Collins' Coastal Pilot's map, also of 1693, as *Anot*. It comes originally from the Gaelic *annoit* meaning old or disused church, the church in this case being Inchbraoch, on the south side of Rossie Island. The ruin was used as a forward sighting-point for mariners coming up river to the harbour, then known as *Stromnay*, later Montrose Harbour. The back sighting-point was also marked on Captain Collins map as *Coults*, perhaps referring to Fullerton which was purchased by the Coutts family as their country seat in the late-seventeenth century.

Heichhame

Had we been passing this way three or four hundred years ago, and seen the river as shown by Captain John Slezer in his well known engraving 'A Prospect of the Town of Montrose' published in 1693, we would have noticed a straggle of huts on the crown of the escarpment, known at the time as *Heichhame* or *Highholme*.

It was a village of fishermen, but unlike their successors at Ferryden, these men fished for salmon in the South Esk, rather than going to sea for white fish. Heichhame must have existed for centuries, but is first documented in the early-seventeenth century when it was part of the Usan estate, which was owned by the Lichton or Leighton family from at least 1260. They sold the estate in 1618 to David, Lord Carnegie. In 1632 a contract was concluded between Sir James

Carnegie of Craig and Alexander Bell of Claylek, whereby 'the said Sir James lets to the said Alexander, the Lands of *Hichome* in the Parish of Inshbreak and the Sheriffdom of Forfar, for 40 bolls oatmeal and 20 bolls beir.'

It passed through a number of hands, usually accompanied by salmon-fishing rights, but dwindled in importance, probably due to being less well-situated for salmon netting than other fishing stations further up river, and to the rising importance of Ferryden. The fishermen of Heichhame finally settled in Montrose in 1776. The 'Lands of *Heighome*' were said in 1805 to lie 'at the mouth of the river Southesk – where landmarks for shipping are marked on Ainslie's map'. These landmarks are still standing. They now also serve to mark the grave of a vanished village.

FERRYDEN

Ferryden itself is represented in Slezer's engraving by only one building, presumably the ferryman's house. The ferry, however, has been there at least since 1178 when the Founding Charter of Arbroath Abbey included the gift of the 'ferry at Munros'. The ferry and its revenues are part of a number of land charters for the estates of Usan, Craig and Rossie in the sixteenth to eighteenth centuries. The village of Ferryden was not founded until the middle of the eighteenth century, when Hercules Ross of Rossie invited families from the Moray Coast to

7 *Ferryden in the 1920s. (Copyright: Angus Council Cultural Services)*

set up a white fishing enterprise. The Welsh traveller, Thomas Pennant, passed through in 1775, and 'crossed the river Southesk in a very good ferry'. Only 20 years later this 'very good ferry' was to be superseded when the first wooden bridge, known as the 'timmer brig' was opened to traffic.

The -*den* part of the name denotes a small wooded valley in Scots and is often used as a descriptive term in Angus and other parts of Lowland Scotland.

STROMNAY

We now come up to the harbour. This area was known to the Vikings, or at least Norse-speaking invaders, as *Stromay* or *Stromnay*. The name, from the Old Norse *strom-a*, which means 'tide-race river', is one of few in the area which can be said to have a Scandinavian origin. A name from the same root is *Stromness* in Orkney.

Stromnay, no doubt a huddle of shacks, was perhaps originally no more than what would later be called an 'entrepot' for Scandinavian traders. It is thought to have been situated near the north end of the present bridge, at the point where Seagate meets the shore. The name *Stromnay* passed out of use in the late-fifteenth century and the area was later called *Fishboats*.

INCHBRAYOCK

We are now passing, on our south side, the island of Inchbrayock, familiarly known as Rossie Island (no longer an island after 1972).

The name *Inchbrayock* or *Inchbraoch* is a Gaelic one, meaning 'the Island of St Brioc' or 'Bhriuc'. *Innis sancta brioc* is mentioned in the medieval Registrum of Aberbrothoc. *Sanct Broc*, whose day was 1 May, is one of the earliest saints in the Calendar. She lived in the fifth century and evidently came from a very pious family. She was the aunt of a much better known saint, St Brigit, known as the Celtic Virgin. There is a place in Cornwall called *St Breock*, and one in Brittany called *St Brieuc*.

A now discredited suggestion, put forward in the nineteenth century, was that the second element -*braoch* came from the Gaelic *breac* meaning 'speckled one', 'trout'. As the river to the west of Rossie Island has long been known as the *Trout Shot* from the abundance of sea-trout caught there, this looked on the face of it like a plausible alternative. But although there are other well-attested *breac* names in Scotland, the earlier mentions of dedication to a saint rule this out.

SALLORK

The settlement on the sandy spit which now accommodates Montrose was up to about 1200 known as *Sallork*, which is thought to come from the Gaelic *sail orc* meaning 'pig's heel'. Apparently the shape of the peninsula was fancied to resemble that appendage, although it is difficult to understand how a medieval peasant could get a bird's eye view to come up with the idea.

Sallork was in existence by the tenth century at the latest, but there is little to suggest that it was a substantial place. Nevertheless, it was important enough to provide funds for royal distribution. We learn from a charter of King Malcolm IV that the church of Restenneth was granted an annual rent of 20*s.* from Sallork for the lighting of its church, together with a teind (tithe) of the King's Ferm at Sallork.

Sallork was Latinised to *Celurca*, or *Selurca*, a name used by the early historian, Hector Boece, who described Montrose in 1526 as

> *Ane strenthie toun, biggit of stane and lyme,*
> *Quhilk callit wes Selurca in the tyme.*

8 April Showers *by William Lamb. (From the collections of the William Lamb Studio)*

MONTROSE

The name *Montrose* is derived from the Gaelic *moine-ros* or *monadh-ros* meaning 'moor on the promontory', which no doubt suited its original appearance, although the name was in fact transferred from the ancient manor of Old Montrose, at the other end of the Basin. The reason for doing so is not clear. It is probable that the Burgh was founded in about 1130 by David I and, as we have seen, it was known for its first 60 years or so as *Sallork*.

So why the change of name? William I came to the throne in 1165, and he seems to have favoured the area for hunting, between periods of harrying the English (and absent-mindedly being captured by them). He did in fact issue at least twenty known charters between 1178 to 1198 at Montrose (*apud Munros*), and although this probably referred to Old Montrose, it was during his reign that the name *Sallork* seems to have passed out of use.

Perhaps this was due merely to personal preference. On the other hand, it has been suggested that *Sallork*, containing the syllable *Sall'* was too reminiscent of the French *sale*, 'dirty', and offended the refined sensibilities of the scribes who had to copy it down. Shades of Victorianism! Blind Harry, the minstrel, writing in about 1470, describes William Wallace landing at Montrose on his return from self-imposed exile on the Continent

> *In Munross haven they brocht him to the land.*
> *Till trew Scots it was a blythe tithand* [happy news].

This and other early documents refer to *Munross, Monros*, or *Munros*, betraying the Gaelic root, but by the seventeenth century the *-t-* has intruded. Adair's map of 1693 is marked *Montross vulgo Monross*, suggesting that only the Philistine of the time left out the *-t-*. The name later evolved to *Montrois*, and finally *Montrose*.

FANCIFUL DERIVATIONS OF 'MONTROSE'

In the late-eighteenth and early-nineteenth century when the first stirrings of gentility began to appear, along with antiquarian societies, thoughts turned to the meaning of the word Montrose.

The name *Montrose* easily suggests the French for 'rose hill', now the name of a well known street in the town. From this the pleasant idea of a hill covered in roses took root, and thence the town motto, '*Mare ditat, rosa decorat*' and the town seal, which depicts a rose.

A French origin for the name was also taken up by the gentleman who suggested that *Montrois* may come from *monts trois*, the three hills in question being *Fort Hill*, *Horologe Hill*, and *Windmill Hill*.

THE PRONUNCIATION OF MONTROSE

Many Scottish place-names have suffered from mispronunciation in the past, being particularly mangled in the mouths of southern newsreaders.

Emphasis on the first syllable, correct for most English names such as *London*, *Manchester*, and *Oxford*, does not work with Gaelic based names where the descriptive element comes second. Hence we have been treated to *Aviemore*, *Inverness*, *Monifeith*, and *Montrose*. But then, perhaps those of us who have difficulty with Salisbury and Cholmondeley should not be too complacent.

TAYOCK BURN

As we pass under the Railway Bridge, we see on our right, at low tide, the Tayock Burn flowing between mud banks. The name *Tayock* has taken many forms over the years. It is spelled as *Touk* and *Teyke* in Provost Rait's Charter of the Lands of Sands in 1670. *Taik* on Adair's map of 1693 and *Take* on Ainslie's of 1794 are other contributions, but the earliest form of the name documented – *Thawhoke* – can be seen in a twelfth-century charter of King David II where the burn serves to denote one of the trading boundaries of the town. This form may indicate that

9 Fisher on the Basin *by William Lamb. (From the collections of the William Lamb Studio)*

the name is composed of the elements *Tay*- possibly a pre-Celtic word for water found in the river names *Tay* and *Thames*, and -*wick* from the Norse word *wic* meaning 'creek or bay'.

CUNNINGAR

At the north-east corner of the Basin beside the road to Brechin stood the *Cunningar of Tayock*, an area of sandy hillocks and whins, still visible in the 1920s. The name comes from *coninger*, a Scots/English word for a rabbit warren. Such warrens were often deliberately established to provide a source of meat. *Coninger* itself comes from *coney*, the Old English word for rabbit. The suffix -*gar* is from the Norse word *garth*, meaning enclosure (from which we get our word garden), or may be a contraction of *earth*. It was here in 1542 that George Wishart, the Protestant martyr, turned back and abandoned a proposed journey to Fife, citing the intervention of the Almighty. His companions later discovered an ambush among the sandhills.

DRONNER'S DYKE

Still visible at low water running east/west across the Basin are the remains of Dronner's (meaning drainer's) Dyke. Its construction began in 1678 after the purchase of the 'Lands of Sands' from the Estate of Dun by a consortium led by Robert Raitt of Snadon. Hopes were high, and in the same year Rev Robert Edward wrote, in *The Shire of Angus*:

> *The Citizens of Montrose, by a dike almost two miles in length which they are raising in the bay in the River Southesk, on the west side of the town, will gain, when the noble work is concluded, about a thousand acres of land. And as the sea will forever be shut out, Montrose may boast of lands, of its own acquisition, so fine as to resemble the Elysian Fields.*

10 *Dronner's Dyke. (Copyright: Neil Werninck)*

The work was almost completed, but a storm and high tide in the winter of 1679 destroyed it, called up, it was said, by Maggie Cowie, a local witch. The eastern end of the dyke can be seen in Slezer's engraving of Montrose published in 1693.

CRAIG

Craig House, which now overlooks us from the south, has claims to being the oldest inhabited building in Angus, perhaps even in Scotland. It has watched the parade of history at least since Edward I of England passed by on 7 July 1296 on his way to accept the surrender of the Scottish Crown by John Balliol, thenceforward known as Toom Tabard, the empty coat. It is shown on Adair's map of 1693, apparently with a surrounding park, and as *Craig House* by Ainslie on his map of 1794. Known at various times as Craig Castle, it was bought in 1505 by Sir Andrew Wood of Largo, Admiral of the Scottish Navy. The name *Craig*, from the Gaelic *creag* meaning rocky hill, is one of the commonest hill names in Angus.

BALGOVE

The farmhouse and steading of Balgove overlook Montrose Basin from a point about halfway between their more imposing neighbours Craig House and the now vanished Rossie Castle.

The name probably comes from the Gaelic *baile*, a farmtoun, the second element being either *gobhain* a smith, or *gobhar* for goat, the whole meaning a smith's steading or a goat farm.

There is a tradition that Balgove was the site of a 'withy house' or prison in medieval times, but there is no documentary evidence to support it. The place of execution was said to have been at Govanhill, about two miles to the southwest, quite a trudge for the condemned.

ROSSIE CASTLE

On our left we are now passing the lands of Rossie, a name whose history stretches back at least to 1245 when Thomas de Rossi had a Charter of the Lands of Rossi from Hugo de

11 *Craig House*

Malherbe. Walter de Rossy, Burgess of Montrose, rendered homage to Edward I in 1296. In 1578, in a charter issued at 'Halyrudehous' to James Rossye, son and heir to David Rossye of that ilk, the lands were said to comprise

> the Lands of Mylntoun of Rossye with the manor and two corn mills thereof, the Hoill Myln [now Holemill], the Lands of Stanelaw, Montboy and moor thereof, Westerton of Rossye and three-quarters of the Mains of Rossye.

The estate was a large and important one until recently, partly due to its also holding, at various times, the other local estates of Craig and Dunninald. Its eminence also arose from its control of the salmon fishing both on its own frontage on the river, and also on the north side, where the Scott family held a firm grip on the burgh fishings for many years.

12 *Rossie Castle in its heyday. (Copyright: Angus Council Cultural Services)*

43

The name *Rossie* comes from the Gaelic *rosach*, 'wooded part or point'. This could fit the topography of the area well enough, although it is possible the original family imported the name from their lands of *Rossie*, in the Carse of Gowrie.

Curiously, a similar transplantation of the name occurred again in much more recent times when Horatio Ross, proprietor of the estate in the nineteenth century and at one time MP for Montrose, sold the property in 1853. He was a well known sportsman and champion shot. Perhaps finding the opportunities for deer-stalking limited in Angus, he moved eventually to Inverness-shire where he died in 1886, at his home – *Rossie Lodge*!

BALDOVIE

A little to the west of the site of Rossie Castle, but much nearer the Basin, we now see Baldovie House. Its earliest mention on maps is as *Baldive* (Edward 1678), then *Balldevie* (1693) and *Baldovie* (from 1794). The name probably comes from the Gaelic *baile domhan* meaning low-lying farm.

On 1 August 1545 it was the birthplace of the great Presbyterian reformer, Andrew Melville, who fought against James VI's determination to introduce bishops to the newly established Church of Scotland. He was prominent at the General Assembly of the Church of Scotland held in Montrose in 1600, when, despite being disbarred from attending by the king, he turned up anyway, and pressed the king again on the subject of bishops. No doubt he felt that in his home town, he ought to have a right to be heard.

MARYTON

Maryton Church is built on a knoll near the foot of Maryton Law and commands a wonderful view of Montrose Basin.

The name was originally applied to *St Mary's Well* which must have been in the vicinity, though no trace of it exists now. However a field on the other side of the Forfar road was called *Ladywell* on an estate map of Old Montrose of 1786. The existence of a church here probably predates that in Montrose, and must have been familiar to King William the Lion who frequented the area on hunting trips. It was he who transferred the church from the patronage of the Brechin diocese to his newly founded abbey at Arbroath in 1178.

ANANIE

Inyaney was the intriguing name of an old estate which 'lay immediately to the West of the Den of Fullerton', according to Rev W R Fraser, author of *St Mary's of Old Montrose*.

The name is derived from the Gaelic words *eoin* and *ach*, 'place of birds'. It has long fallen into disuse, but it conjures up a picture appropriate to our present-day interest in ornithological matters. The *Lands of Inyaney* first appear in the record when King William the Lion, on a visit to Montrose between 1178 and 1197, confirmed a grant to the Gatekeeper (porter) or Constable of Montrose Castle, a man named Crane, who had a heritable fee of the estate. His son, Swayne and grandson Simon succeeded him. Simon was blessed with five daughters from two wives, but no sons. Daughters, under the laws of the time, did not have an automatic title to the inheritance. Nevertheless, they made a joint claim on the land. A barons' assize had to be held in 1261 to decide the question, and came down in favour of the five ladies, resoundingly named in the documents as Margareta, Agnes, Swannoch, Christiana, and Mariota.

About 60 years later, in 1328, the estate again appears, this time in royal charter granted by Robert the Bruce, by then almost at the end of his reign, to Walter Schaklok who, in the same year, sold on one third of his *Lands of Inieney* to Henry de Rossy, owner of the neighbouring estate. In 1629 the young man, later to be Marquis of Montrose, was married, at age 17, to Magdalene Carnegie, daughter of the 1st Earl of Southesk. The marriage contract included liferent of one third of the *Lands of Ananie* as it was then spelled.

The Old Manse of Maryton is now called *Annfield*. Could this be a faint echo of it's past?

Fullerton

We can just about see Fullerton Farm from the Basin.

The name means fuller's or fowler's farm. It was presumably named when in 1327, Robert I gifted lands in Maryton to Geoffrey, his chief falconer for Angus. He took the name *Fullerton* for his land and for himself. The Fullerton family connection with the estate continued until 1447 when it was sold to the Crawmount family. In 1629 it was included in the marriage contract already referred to between the future Marquis of Montrose and Magdalen Carnegie, daughter of the 1st Earl of Southesk.

Old Montrose

The name *Montrose* originated here, and it suits the description of 'moor on a promontory' very well. Remembering that the Basin in earlier times extended farther east (the Lurgies, for instance, being reclaimed only in the nineteenth century), the castle of Old Montrose must have stood on a knoll or promontory amid marshy ground in a position which gave clear views of the Basin. Along with Dun, it also guarded the entrance to the South Esk from sea-borne invaders.

The Lurgies

The Lurgies is a partly swampy area to the west of the river as it enters the Basin. It was reclaimed in the 1820s when Sir James Carnegie of Old Montrose built embankments on the south-west side of the South Esk. His efforts were only partially successful as the area was still inundated at spring tides and even so, the harbour trustees were unhappy about the possible reduction in tidal flow in the harbour.

The name may be of Gaelic origin, from *luirge* meaning a 'shank-like strip of land', but if so, it must have been named long before any reclamation, as the Gaelic language was no longer then spoken hereabouts. Perhaps it referred to a feature which was obvious in the original condition of the land.

DRUM OF DUN

The farm of Drum of Dun farm stands midway between Dun and Old Montrose. It was formerly known as Drum of Old Montrose, but due to the South Esk changing its course in the early-nineteenth century, it found itself on the north rather than the south side of the river. In Ainslie's map of 1799 it is called *Drum of Maryton*. But still as *Drum of Old Montrose* it is

13 *Bridge of Dun*

found on Blackadder's plan of 1833 of the marches between Old Montrose and Dun, which was drawn up as evidence in a dispute between the landowners as a result of the river changing course. It still lies within Maryton parish.

Drum comes from the Gaelic *druim* meaning ridge. As there is no discernible ridge hereabouts, the word may in this case have been used to denote the boundary between the estates of Dun and Old Montrose.

SLUNKS

The Slunks is a marshy area near the north shore of the South Esk as it enters Montrose Basin. It occupies an area to the east of Drum of Dun farm, which was the former course of the river prior to its change in the eighteenth century described on maps as 'sea greens'. *Slunk* is a very evocative Scots word meaning 'mire' or 'quagmire'. A salmon pool further up the South Esk is known as *The Slunk*, meaning in this case a ditch.

As we enter the South Esk proper, we can look back northward to see the splendid sweep of the north side of the Basin.

House of Dun

Adam's splendid building can be easily seen from the Basin. It replaces an earlier castle, which stood a little further west and, with its counterpart the castle of Old Montrose on the south bank of the river, commanded a strategic view of the Basin.

The Barony of Dun is one of the oldest and most prestigious in the area, having been given to John de Hastings by King William the Lion in the late-twelfth century. By far its most famous holders were the Erskine family, which produced a number of figures prominent on the Scottish scene.

Dun, meaning fortified hill in Gaelic, is unusual in that it gives us the unadorned form of the name, rather than having the addition of a qualifying element such as in *Dunblane* or *Dunbar*. It is found in the estate of *Dun* and its various dependant farms such as *Mains* (the demesne or principal farm), *Fordhouse* (the farm at the ford), *Leys* (the grass park), and the now lost *Crook of Dun*.

Broomley

Broomley, from early times part of the Barony of Dun, was included in the lands given to the See of Brechin by Sir John Erskine in 1409. It was later returned to Dun.

The name is almost self-explanatory, from *broom* with *-ley*, as in *Leys of Dun*, meaning grassland.

Ecclesjohn (Langley Park)

The spot was originally called *Ecclesjohn*, or *Egglisjohn*, from the Gaelic *eaglais-* meaning church, and the saint to whom it was dedicated, *John*. It was a charge attached to Brechin cathedral and described in the Middle Ages as 'of auld ane chapell erectit for pilgrimage'. The name was changed to *Langley Park* in 1787 when the estate was bought by George Ogilvy who named it after his estate in the West Indies.

Kirkdoorkeys

This site is mentioned in several manuscripts as being part of the estate of Dun, and later of Langley Park. The exact location of this intriguingly named place is unknown, as is the derivation of the name.

Gilrivie

Gilrivie farm lies at the north-western corner of Montrose Basin. Within its boundaries are the remains of a Roman camp, visible in aerial photographs taken under suitable conditions. The name is of Gaelic origin, but its meaning is obscure.

Glenskenno

In 1576 this glen was described as *Skannack*, later as *Shanno*. The name may come from the Gaelic, *sgeann-ach* a clean, neat place, or *sgann-ach* a herding, or drove place. However, in 1656 we find a location named 'Glasker, commonly called Glaskenno, with mill, etc and the Lands of Sands of Northsyde of the water of Southesk' This might suggest an alternative derivation.

PUGESTON

This is one of a large number of names ending in -ton, from the Anglo-Saxon, meaning farm, which often have a personal name as the defining element, in this case possibly a gentleman by the name of Poggi or Poca, which is a known Scandinavian personal name.

NEWBIGGING

Newbigging Farm, lying about halfway along the north side of the Basin, is marked on Ainslie's map of 1794. It is mentioned in 1637 as being in the possession of Alexander Erskine, having previously belonged to other members of the Erskine family. In the seventeenth century it became part of the Hedderwick Estate gifted, on his marriage, to David Scott, one of the six sons of James Scott the Elder, of Logie.

In 1819 it was bought by James Cruickshank of Langley Park. The lands of Newbigging included the mill, which can be seen on Paterson's print of Langley Park. The name is from Scots and simply means 'new building'. It is one of many throughout the country bearing the same name, most of which, curiously enough, are of fairly ancient origin.

HEDDERWICK

Hedderwick lies near the head of the Tayock Burn, on the north side of the Basin. It is one of the oldest estates in the area, and may possibly have been granted by King William the Lion to his brother David, Earl of Huntingdon in the twelfth century.

The name has changed little in pronunciation over the years, but has produced a plethora of spelling variations, ranging from Haddirvyk in 1340 through Hatyrwic and Hederweik to its present version.

The origin of the name has been the subject of some controversy. The Hedder- element, meaning heather is common to many Germanic languages. However -wick, has alternative meanings. In the south of Scotland and in England its use in place-names derives from the Old English word for a homestead or village, as in Hawick, Prestwick, and further south, in Sandwich. To describe a place such as Hedderwick as a homestead would be perfectly acceptable were it not for the fact that no other -wic names appear so far north. Perhaps a more likely contender might be the Norse term -wic, meaning bay or creek, as in Wick itself, Lerwick, and Brodick.

The Tayock Burn, although docile and contained now, with the progress of farming practice and the well-attested silting up of the Basin, is no doubt very different from its youthful exuberance at the time of the naming of Hedderwick. The likelihood of a Norse derivation is reinforced by the presence of other Norse place-names in the vicinity, such as Stromnay, and Grimsby at Arbroath (found as far back as 1524).

Therefore the most likely derivation for *Hedderwick* may be 'heathery creek', although the possibility that it is an outlying example of an Old English *-wic* name, and hence means 'heather farm' cannot be ignored.

BORROWFIELD

Borrowfield lies on the upper reaches of the Tayock burn. It appears on Edward's map of 1678 as *Borrofeild*, and on Blackadder's map of 1825 as *Burrowfield*. The name probably means 'field or farm belonging to the burgh'.

The estate has been in existence since medieval times, being mentioned as belonging to the Graham family before 1408 when it was sold to Alexander Gardyne. In 1615 it came into the possession of Hercules Tailzeour, whose family held it until 1806.

That completes our circumnavigation of Montrose Basin, perhaps rekindling an interest in the origin of the names of places which may have become so familiar as to be unremarked.

4   Montrose Basin in Prehistory

Until the withdrawal of the glaciers from Scotland after the last Ice Age it would not have been possible for humans to live in the area. By perhaps 7000BC life here may have been tolerable as roaming people followed wild animals, part of their natural diet, into the warming areas further north.

Once a climate akin to the current one had re-established itself, the local area would have been attractive to human inhabitants. At this time people lived their lives as 'hunter-gatherers', a semi-nomadic existence following food sources. The South Esk estuary would have provided an abundant natural larder – which included one of the more important salmon fisheries in Scotland, shell-fish beds, sea birds for meatier dishes, and a broad range of local plants, including seaweeds, which would have supplemented this diet. Good freshwater supplies and trees around the river would have provided not just fuel, but cover and forage for natural game that could be hunted. When the topography changed further, so that the Basin itself was created, then even larger numbers of migrant birds would have used the area (as now), providing an exceptional food source. All these resources could develop and be exploited away from the risks of the sea.

So far no trace of these earliest inhabitants has yet been discovered, not least because there has been little detailed fieldwork to search for them. However, with their mobile lives, based in tents or other fragile shelters and with the majority of their possessions made out of biodegradable natural resources, evidence of their passing would be slight. Generally searches for earlier sites of this type would have to be undertaken in areas believed to be favoured occupation sites. Many of these would have been close to the sources of food and thus adjacent to rivers or on beach sites. But there is another problem: Montrose lies on the east coast of Scotland and when a *tsunami* (see Geology chapter) hit north east Scotland in about 5000BC, it inundated the local coast and South Esk valley for some distance upstream. Silt and gravel shifted during this tidal wave buried the earlier ground surfaces on lower lying land effectively hiding all earlier occupation sites.

When we talk of the prehistoric periods we are referring to an occupation period of over 8000 years of gradual development. The population would have grown and changed, agricultural activity would have been introduced, and increasingly sophisticated industrial processes developed. Social structures, religion, burial practices, agriculture, industry, housing and many other things would have evolved. Our (albeit still limited) understanding of things in these periods of the past has to be derived from the physical traces the people left behind. Archaeology involves piecing together fragments that remain, comparing these with others from elsewhere that may be relevant, and then trying to interpret what they mean.

So what are the main pieces of the archaeological jigsaw puzzle which collectively allow a picture of the past to be built? There are the monuments that survive and the finds that are either discovered by chance or are derived from archaeological field survey or excavation. There can be aerial photographic evidence revealing buried sites. There is antiquarian tradition of sites or finds that were made in the past, plus more recent evidence from archaeological excavation. There is also the evidence to be derived from place-names.

PREHISTORIC OCCUPATION

Because the Montrose Basin area has been relatively heavily occupied since the prehistoric period, with much of it under arable farming, few early archaeological sites now survive as above ground monuments in areas favourable for ploughing. The ones that do are all apparently barrows, or burial mounds. Maryton Law survives on the south side of the Basin, and another lay at Fordhouse of Dun. Fordhouse may be a lucky survivor because it was located in what later became woodland of the Dun estate. Maryton Law, extremely prominent, may have survived because it was used as an important land marker in subsequent years and probably also a sight line for determining areas of ownership on the Basin itself. Gallows Knowe, the enigmatic mound on the east side of the drive leading to the House of Dun, may indeed have been the mound for a later gallows as its name suggests, but it has been suggested that it is also another early burial mound.

The other physical source of evidence of the past is early finds. These are important indicators of the activities of people in the past, but they are also of course used for dating sites. For the Basin area we have both individual chance finds and others derived from archaeological fieldwork. With the passing of time, generally only the most robust of finds survive – stone, or more rarely, metalwork. Even rarer are ceramic finds, but several excavations have shown the style of what might have been expected. No early finds of organic materials – wood, bone,

14 *Maryton Law, showing the burial mound at its summit*

leather, basketry for example have been identified so far, although there is the possibility that early waterlogged sites with precisely such objects may yet be discovered. Some of the finds held in the local or national museums have been gathered over nearly two centuries. Larger or more exceptional finds, such as polished stone axes or complete bronze swords, always attracted attention. Smaller or seemingly less interesting finds tend even now to be reported only by those with a specific knowledge or interest in the past.

ANTIQUARIAN REPORTS

Antiquarian reports of sites or finds fill some of the gaps in our knowledge, although again only certain types of sites will be reported. The 'Old Statistical Account' of *c*1790 specifically asked the authors from each parish to report on antiquities of interest, and as a result we have early reports of 'cist burials' in the Dun area made in the latter part of the eighteenth century. Interestingly, this was the time when there were major agricultural improvements in the area and larger areas of upland land would have been brought into arable farming. This would have led to the disturbance and discovery of many sites. Montrose itself had one of the earliest antiquarian societies in Scotland when it was established in the 1836. It built its own museum to house its collections. The annual written report starts to provide information on sites discovered that might otherwise be lost, such as the report of early burials under the new railway being built through Balwyllo in the 1850s.

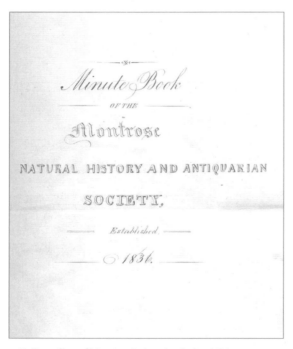

15 *Proceedings of Montrose Antiquarian Society 1836*

The study of place-names may also indicate early sites, or occupation, in the area. But the interpretation of names, which have passed through many transformations from their original descriptive meaning, is not easy. This study is dealt with in more detail in the previous chapter. But the combination of place-names and other evidence may well prove fruitful as well as opening the eyes of researchers to the possibility of specific sites that could be confirmed by other evidence. The quetion of whether there was a *dun*, or early fort, at Dun is just one example of this.

AERIAL PHOTOGRAPHY

A much more recent study that is transforming our knowledge of the area is aerial photographic research. Very simply, buried archaeological sites may affect the way crops above them grow. With a combination of the correct crops and suitable weather conditions during the growing season, distinct 'crop-marks' will be formed that are visible from the air. Fortunately the north and west hinterlands around Montrose Basin have been recognised as an exceedingly good area for photographic results. Some sites are so diagnostic that they can be broadly dated without other supporting information – Pictish square barrows and the Roman camp are cases in point of this – and immediately designated as nationally important. As the density of important sites is so high, regular trips are made into the area, and more details of these early sites emerge.

ARCHAEOLOGICAL INVESTIGATIONS

There have been two modern excavations on prehistoric sites and both have thrown important light on the area in the past. Both were undertaken for slightly different purposes. At Maryton Law trial excavations funded by Historic Scotland were undertaken to test the level of damage to the mound being caused by rabbits. The date of the mound was clearly established for the first time and important Bronze Age finds made, in spite of the disturbance. At Fordhouse of Dun a barrow had already been partially damaged by ancient quarrying and trees and more rabbit damage was occurring. It was decided that further controlled de-struction through excavation would be justified by important finds. This barrow proved to be extremely intriguing, re-used over many centuries from the Neolithic through the Bronze Age, and then re-used again for a possible Viking burial more than fifteen hundred years later. The individual grave-goods proved to be extensive and some exceptional for both the area and nationally.

Over time sites will inevitably be destroyed or damaged, so we cannot expect the total survival that would allow us to have the fullest picture of any period in the past. Some of the information

16 *Fordhouse burial*

sources we are using, such as antiquarian reports, are garbled or incomplete, not having been written for the use of researchers in the future. Reports of 'cists' clearly refer to stone lined graves; equally clearly we have to recognise that this type of burial practice occurred from the Bronze Age through to the Pictish period, for maybe 3500 years, so closer dating is not possible without more diagnostic finds. In spite of these challenges and difficulties, the combination of access to all the sources above allows a broad picture to emerge for each phase of the prehistoric and a taste of that is given below.

MESOLITHIC TIMES (PRE-8000BC–3500BC)

As previously mentioned, sites from the earliest occupation of the Basin area have still not been discovered. This time is referred to as the Mesolithic. The people at this time would have been hunter-gatherers. The natural food resources of the Basin area could have supported quite a substantial number of people for much of the year. The diversity and extent of these resources also meant that groups would not necessarily have had to hunt in such a broad area as those people who lived in the less favourable areas, such as the higher land inland for example. In the earlier periods they would have lived in temporary huts or tents, or possibly in caves and rock shelters if they were available, by the latter part of the period they would have been moving towards a more settled existence.

A nomadic lifestyle means that it is difficult to retain or transport large quantities of belongings. But the people would almost certainly have carried their belongings in bags made of skin or possibly in woven baskets. Tools would have been of wood, bone or stone. Without the discovery and excavation of a well-preserved site, the likelihood of recovering most of these types of evidence is extremely slim. The one exception to this might be the stone tools. The diagnostic stone tools for this period are microliths, tiny chips of stone or flint. These would no doubt have originally been mounted in wooden frames or handles, probably with some type of gum or glue. But because microliths are so small, sometimes as little as a few millimetres long, they are not easy to spot. They will undoubtedly be discovered in the Basin area in due course, but it is likely to require intensive archaeological survey. Each field would have to be walked slowly and checked carefully for finds of this type.

NEOLITHIC ADVANCES (3500BC–2500BC)

The next period, in archaeological terms, is called the Neolithic. This is defined by a considerably different lifestyle to the one described above, although it should be noted that there could have been a considerable period of evolution from one to the other. The Neolithic is defined by a number of things. These include organised animal husbandry, the use of arable farming – which inevitably means a more settled lifestyle, with semi-permanent buildings – and the production and use of a broad range of tools (including pottery for the first time) that might be traded over many hundred of miles. And most particularly by the building, and use, of large monuments for ritual, or funerary, purposes. Many of these sites and finds are quite distinct and so are much easier to identify by archaeologists and researchers. By comparing sites and evidence we can start to build a much more detailed picture of how these people lived. The evidence for the Basin area is still limited, but collectively the sources cover the full area of the survey and thus are complementary. By comparing what we have with more detailed, but similar, site knowledge from elsewhere, a clearer picture starts to emerge.

The first Neolithic finds reported from the area were a series of polished stone axes. These can be extremely finely made tools. We know that many were derived, and traded, from major quarries or factories scattered around Britain, supplemented by others manufactured from more local sources. Stone must have been quarried and cut into rough blanks. These would then have been rubbed, or polished, to give a smooth surface. Each one must have taken many hours to work. They are referred to as axes because of their shape and some may indeed have been capable of chopping, but this may of course not have been their original purpose at all. That remains to be determined, although there are suspiciously large clusters reported around some ritual sites. A number of the axes are held in Montrose Museum, and their findspots point to a dispersed Neolithic population or activity. Several finds have been reported from Montrose itself, another on Scurdie Ness (where there have been persistent antiquarian reports of old 'defences'), and one 'in the Basin'. One was found at Hillside during drainage works, and one found when the Bridge of Dun was being built. The bridge lies close to an earlier river crossing that has always been regarded as hazardous at certain times of the year. Perhaps some traveller (or his belongings) came to grief here 5000 years ago.

Axes, however, are in some ways exceptional, and might travel from their original position after Neolithic times. They are sometimes found on other later sites and there is of course the folklore tradition of placing one 'up the lum' to prevent lightning striking your house. So if we want to track down sites that were occupied in the Neolithic we need to track down more mundane tools that are still where they were originally used and discarded. Neolithic people would have used a broad range of stone and flint tools for a range of purposes. There are flint spears and arrowheads, probably used for hunting, but potentially available for other more aggressive activities as well. But there would have been a broad range of utilitarian tools such as blades and scrapers used for the preparation of skins for instance. Occasional finds have been reported from around the area – several at the Old Montrose end of the Basin and another more recently from a garden in Hillside. Archaeological fieldwalking in the Bonnyton Farm area produced a broad range of flint/stone in an area where aerial photographs indicate disturbance, so there might well have been an occupation site here.

A Cursus Discovered

Aerial photographs seem to indicate that within the Basin Survey area, at the western end lying across Powys and Old Montrose estates, lay one of the more enigmatic Neolithic monuments – a cursus. A long linear site, it is now visible on photographs as a pair of roughly parallel ditches running across several fields. A later circular feature, possibly a defended enclosure

17 *The cursus at Old Montrose*

of some type has been built into one end. Nobody really knows what these features were used for, so they are often described as 'ritual', not least because later sites of certain types, such as burial mounds, tend to cluster around them. This would indicate that a cursus might survive as a recognisable element in the landscape for a considerable length of time – perhaps several millennia. This may be the case at Old Montrose where a series of round barrows which might be as early as the Bronze Age (*c*2500–800BC) are also visible on photographs clustered close to the cursus. More unusually though, several square barrows are also visible. These are generally thought to date from the Iron Age/Pictish period. It should be noted that one of the square barrows can be seen within the confines of the cursus itself, indicating that it might finally have gone out of use, or local awareness. It has been suggested that longer cursuses may be processional ways, but equally the ditches may have enclosed structures that are now gone. Very few have been examined in detail, but one (the famous Cursus at Long Crichel in Dorset) revealed very little internally. Ironically, clusters of Neolithic polished axes were found outside it instead.

It has been suggested by one researcher that the Old Montrose cursus might have formed the centre of a wider ritual landscape, with a cluster of other important sites around it. Locally only one other site that is definitely of the Neolithic period has been identified, and that was revealed during the excavations of the barrow at Fordhouse of Dun. The final report had not been published at the time of writing this chapter, so the interpretation given here has been based on interim statements by the excavator (Edwina Proudfoot). The main structure of the barrow was Bronze Age but during the course of excavation, in addition to Bronze Age burials, the remains of a timber structure were identified under the mound. Ditches on either side contained traces of imported stone types that are normally dated to the Neolithic. A full explanation of what this might once have been has to await the excavator's full report. However, in the Neolithic period we could expect to see large 'chambered cairns', such as the one that survives at Fasque. They were often roughly rectangular with a forecourt. A stone-built central chamber would run from this and sometimes there were side chambers, all covered by a long stone cairn. Human remains and other finds would be placed in these cairns, but they undoubtedly had a broader function than just burial. It is possible that this is a rarer timber chamber variant here, important enough to be re-used and adapted later.

Another monument awaiting more detailed assessment is a large circular feature identified on aerial photographs to the south of Langley Park. It is suggested that this might be a Neolithic henge. These ritual monuments are still poorly understood, but are defined by an external bank outside an enclosing ditch both with a very narrow entrance. Some, on excavation, appear to have had upright internal timbers or standing stones, whose purpose is still obscure. The Langley Park monument has a ring of internal holes that might have once held such posts.

BRONZE AGE FINDS

In the Bronze Age some people would be buried in barrows (burial mounds) and these were generally round in shape and defined by an external ditch. When we refer to burials, some were indeed regular inhumations and others were cremation burials. Often each burial would

18 *Beakers*

be accompanied by grave goods, with cremations placed in pots. Other finds, sometimes deliberately broken, might be placed in the mound. Fordhouse of Dun turned out some exceptional results in spite of previous damage. In addition to the earlier Neolithic finds under the barrow and later re-use in the Norse period, the remains of 38 separate Bronze Age ceramic pots were identified. There would have been one primary burial and then the barrow would have been re-used for later interments occurring over many hundreds of years. The pots (which are used for phasing of burials by archaeologists) would have been handmade using the coil technique, individually decorated and then fired in small kilns. Thirty eight pots from one barrow is extremely unusual, but among them was the largest Bronze Age pot so far recovered from Scotland. Pots could either have held cremated remains, or may have held grave goods such as food or drink that does not now survive. In Fordhouse barrow there were both types – decorated 'beakers' and pots buried with cremations, often upside down. Again, uniquely in Scotland, a cremation was accompanied by not one, but three pots of varying types and sizes.

Maryton Law, another barrow which forms a very distinct feature on the local skyline, was not totally excavated, but it was possible to assess whether this site was a medieval castle motte as claimed by one local historian (it wasn't). Its original dimensions – 34 metres in diameter and a height of perhaps 6 metres over bedrock – were determined. Old mapping shows that the site had already been affected by quarrying in the eighteenth and nineteenth centuries and rabbit damage was shown to be quite severe. This effectively meant that burials and grave goods had been disturbed. The trenches were restricted to these areas of disturbance and 17 sherds of Bronze Age pottery were recovered. Some were of beakers dated to 2600–1800BC, one of which was a 'short beaker' which it was suggested would normally accompany a child or infant, others were from a 'food vessel', dated from 1700–1150BC. Other finds were also recovered – a series of flint tools and the remains of hazelnuts, hinting at normal Bronze Age life. But again there was another extremely unusual find – part of a large clear crystal. This would not have occurred naturally on the site and so must have been deliberately imported to the area, probably to be used as a rare and unusual grave deposit.

19 *Rock crystal found at Maryton Law. (Copyright: Angus Council Cutural Services)*

Again ordinary occupation sites of this period have not been definitely identified yet. On the aerial photographs a number of ditched enclosures can be seen around the Basin, and it is likely that a number of these may be Bronze Age. It is possible to see the external ditches of these sites, but they are likely to have enclosed house sites, or possibly they could have been used as stock enclosures. Fieldwork will be necessary to confirm this and indeed link all our information sources more closely together.

Apart from the pottery from the excavated sites, occasional chance finds of the Bronze Age period are reported. Stone and flint tools were still used and there are reports of these from around the Basin area. The most diagnostic finds are the rarer metal finds, bronze because iron was not yet in use. During the nineteenth century two Bronze Age swords were reported, with one recovered during the demolition of buildings in the area of the port. Swords are generally believed to be introduced quite late in the period and these perhaps date to *c*800BC. Several earlier bronze axes, or palstaves, reported from a wider area are in Montrose Museum, but apparently confusion has developed over which ones came from where. However, a press report from the 1930s clearly indicates that one 'looped and socketed' axe came from road repairs on Rossie Island.

MR POCOCKE'S DISCOVERY

Undoubtedly the most important Bronze Age finds from the Montrose area were discovered in the latter part of the eighteenth century. If something similar was discovered today it would be regarded as a nationally important find. Only the sketchiest description survives included in the travelogue of a traveller Richard Pococke who was searching for the site of the medieval Blackfriars. We are told that

> *enquiring for the convent, I was informed it was a little to the north of the town at Muir Montrose, which is a house belonging to Mr Kennedy, where foundations of buildings have been discovered and under the threshold of the door an urn with a utensil of gold worth 12 pounds which from the description answers to a fibula in this shape the like of which has often been found in Ireland.*

The valuation is not entirely without relevance as this indicates that the piece was almost certainly melted down for its gold content, 12 pounds for bullion would have been a considerable sum of money and suggests a weighty object. No illustrations of this 'fibula', or brooch, apparently survive, but as it has been paralleled with material from Ireland there have been suggestions that it was a heavy, decorated armlet with flared terminals. The reference to an accompanying 'urn' points to another possible Bronze Age burial site. Needless to say there is no description or illustration of the more lowly pot.

What else is now lost? It is possible that another site once located north of the town could have been a standing stone. The name 'standing stone field' was used for one of the town fields until the seventeenth century. A subsequent house in the area was also called 'Stonefield'. It is possible that this was a later boundary marker stone, but equally it could date back to the

Bronze Age when individual stones were raised, or formed part of stone circles. This site has probably been completely lost now, but some stones in the Bronze Age were decorated with either cup or ring marks – engraved designs. Two cup-marked stones are reported as being built into an old cottage in the woods north of Dun. It is possible that re-used marked stones will be discovered in due course. DH Edwards the Brechin journalist writing in 1899 refers to a tumulus still pointed out on the Links immediately north east of the town. He said that this may have been where victims of the 1648–9 plague were buried. Was this true? An earlier antiquarian report of 1851 by Daniel Wilson, in *The Prehistoric Annals of Scotland*, has a chapter discussing the form of skulls from early burials across Scotland. One reference to the burial under the Old Kirk tower, almost certainly refers incorrectly to a medieval burial. But there is also another reference to a skull in Edinburgh from a tumulus in Montrose, seemingly yet another otherwise unlocated burial mound.

THE IRON AGE

By perhaps 800BC iron tools would have been coming in to use. And although this has led to the classification of a new period, the Iron Age, it is probable that for the majority of the residents life may have continued almost exactly as previously. It has been suggested that there may have been defensive sites or forts at Dun and possibly on Scurdie Ness. Enigmatic aerial photographic evidence of the Bonnyton area may point to a large defended enclosure hereabouts, but confirmatory evidence is still lacking. It is probable that at least some of the scattered ditched enclosures around the Basin visible on aerial photographs were also of this period and represent enclosed farmsteads or similar. We can be certain that there were substantial numbers of Iron Age residents in the Basin area, but distinctive monuments are few and far between and modern excavated evidence is still lacking. One monument, however, that is attributed definitely to the Iron Age is the square barrow. We have no surviving upstanding monuments, but we do have evidence of the defining ditches on aerial photographs. So far these have been spotted in only one location – at the west end of the Basin, close to the cursus that runs between Old Montrose and Powys. One lies outside the cursus another nearby within it; slightly further away there is yet another. It is also possible that others that once lay in the area have been removed by the road- and field-boundaries in the area. However, even more intriguingly, they are surrounded by a scattering of round barrows and there is possibly also a large unenclosed cemetery with dozens of burials nearby. Recent excavations at Lunan Bay of a mixed square and round barrow cemetery proved that both types could be of this period. Is this the case at Old Montrose, or do we instead have a burial area that continued in use for many centuries?

More ring ditches are visible in the fields at Balwyllo, close to the railway. These can almost certainly be linked to other sites reported in the nineteenth century. One of the few cases of local archaeological finds reported in the Montrose Natural History and Antiquarian Society

Journal (1867) refers to discoveries in this area and even more helpfully we have an illustration to help explain the text.

> In the course of excavation at Balwyllo, by the Caledonian Railway Company, several ancient graves have been laid bare. They were found to lie nearly E–W and from 6–9 feet in length about 4 feet deep in gravel. Three of them contained a quantity of incinerated bones and wood charcoal. In one of them a fragment of ancient urn and a piece of iron about 8 inches in length. Another contained neither bones nor wood ashes and was surrounded by a circle 35 feet in diameter dug into the gravel about 1 foot deep. Also a trench and also a circular hole 18 inches wide and same depth on the south side of the grave. There appears to have been a cairn over both the grave and the hole.

The report of the iron find means that we are definitely dealing with at least some burials later than the Bronze Age here. Iron unfortunately survives very badly in most archaeological deposits, but a description of a piece 8 inches long suggests that the excavators may have recovered the remains of grave goods, possibly part of a sword blade or similar.

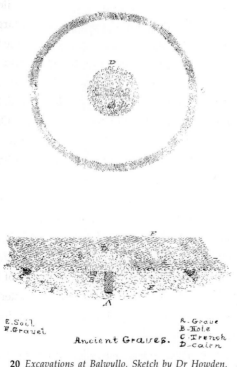

E.Soil.
F.Gravel.

Ancient Graves.

A .Grave
B .Hole
C .Trench
D .Cairn

20 *Excavations at Balwyllo. Sketch by Dr Howden.*
(Copyright: Angus Council Cultural Services)

IDENTIFICATION FROM THE AIR

If there are graves for the dead then there must have been occupation sites for the living too, the difficulty (in the absence of excavation) is working out which of the sites identified from aerial photography belong to this period. A Roman camp of the first century AD has been identified near Gilrivie (see chapter below). Aerial photographs of the area seem to show a number of circular features both nearby and in the camp area itself. These could well be the visible remains of large circular huts of the type that would have been occupied by the native population both before and after the Roman presence in the area. Searching between the lines of the accounts of the Roman invasion, it is possible to see that north east Scotland supported a large population at this time. Although the first Roman invasion of the area was relatively short lived, it carried with it a deliberate scorched earth policy, and reports of horrendous numbers of native casualties. It is suggested from evidence from sites in Aberdeenshire that some areas still bore the marks of invasion on their agricultural record over a century later. We do not have comparative evidence for the Basin area yet, but the picture might prove to be slightly different. Just as the natural wealth of the area might have attracted the invasion force in the first place, so it might allow the more rapid re-building and recovery of the local economy after their departure.

If this was Southern Scotland or England then the Iron Age would be ended with the Roman invasion. But in the Montrose area although the Roman impact may have been severe, the natives (later called the Picts) continued to occupy the area for many hundred of years subsequently and their descendants eventually became the medieval inhabitants. We can expect many things to have continued largely unchanged for long periods, until the introduction of one of the most major cultural impacts – Christianity.

5   The Romans in Montrose

At the time of the first Roman invasion of northern Scotland in the first century AD we can assume that the Montrose Basin area had been settled for many millennia. The community was probably stable, relatively populous and wealthy as the residents made use of all the local resources. By 79–80 when the invasion of southern Scotland began, locals (living in the port area) would undoubtedly have heard stories about the Romans. Some would undoubtedly have been apocryphal; others may have been substantially true as Roman activity in England would have triggered exile for some from their invaded lands. Roman traders may also have been seen off the Montrose coastal waters – their exotic trade goods may have been welcomed, until it became obvious that such traders might be the fore-runners of the Roman army and were actively checking out the local population and their harbours and defences.

In spite of such strategies, the politics that led to the invasion of Scotland had little to do with the activities of the native people and all to do with the politics of the Roman Empire itself. But the locals would have had to deal with the short-term consequences of a hostile invasion force in their area and the longer-term consequences of the major disruption caused to the economy and stability of the eastern coast for at least a century after.

So who were the Romans? Once an Italian city state, they had expanded to become a huge military empire covering all of Italy, much of North Africa, large areas of the Middle East, all of the northern Mediterranean fringes into the Balkans, Spain, much of Germany and France and more recently England and Wales. The Empire had been expanding over several centuries through a combination of political intrigue and military conquest. There was an extremely large standing army and this (and indeed the other structures and economy of the empire itself) could only be maintained through continual military expansion. This military activity provided loot and prisoners who could be conscripted as auxiliary military levies in the short term and occupied lands that could be taxed in the longer term.

SURVIVING EVIDENCE OF THE ROMANS IN MONTROSE

Knowledge of the Roman invasion of Scotland is gradually becoming more detailed through archaeological research. But the evidence for the Roman presence in the Montrose area is

21 *Roman ring*

still very sparse. There is a scattering of Roman finds from across the Basin area, any of which taken alone could be attributed to simple trade. On display in Montrose Museum is a gold

Roman ring of perhaps the second century AD with a banded agate stone found at Usan. A further intaglio of the first to second century AD, discovered without its ring in which it would have been set, has been carved with a classical Roman design of a bearded man leaning against a tree, possibly a goatherd with a dog sitting at his feet. Excavations at the native settlement at Lunan Bay recovered pieces of a fine Roman glass bowl. And from Montrose itself, one solitary sherd of Roman pottery has been reported to the museum. But set against this has been the discovery of the still unique find of a Roman military camp at Gilrivie, near Dun, now believed to have been used by the Roman navy.

22 *Roman intaglio*

THE ROMANS REACH DUN

The Camp was discovered by aerial photography by the leading archaeological aerial photographer of the early 1970s, Keith St Joseph. In 1973 he examined the site and reported the discovery of one sherd of Samian pottery. Samian pottery was actually made in France, not Samos, but it is a very distinctive fine ware traded widely across the Roman Empire and into Britain. This sherd could be dated to roughly AD70–90 and thus tied the camp to the first century AD military campaign known about from written Roman sources and archaeological evidence from elsewhere. The camp, which covers about 8 acres, lies on the north side of the Basin south of the old railway line. It lay on the east side of an inlet of the Basin (now infilled), and less than 200 metres from the original Basin edge.

Its location immediately led to the suggestion that it was planned to be supplied by sea. It is interesting that it lies on the north side of the Basin, as all subsequent port areas other than at the river mouth have been located on the south where the river channels for access are deeper and more secure, especially at times of low tide. Perhaps the north side was favoured for ease of access to other military bases located inland. Perhaps the South Esk formed a political boundary at this time and it was considered politically more expedient to be located on this side, rather than the topographically more favourable south. Or possibly the Romans were taking over an earlier portage area. One of the estates a little to the east was known in medieval times as Hedderwick, this name is possibly derived from Norse with the '-wick' element suggesting an inlet, or possibly even a small township. This more sheltered area may have been more important than the town area itself at this early stage.

Very little of the camp is visible on the ground itself, except for the occasional soil or crop mark created over the ditches and internal features. The Brechin Road now passes right through it and several of the roadside cottages lie within it, so its site is easy to locate once you know that it is there. Fortunately when the railway was built in the nineteenth century by avoiding the inlet they avoided damaging the camp, missing it by less than fifty metres. So it still lies beneath the surface, available for future research, and standing as a testament to the violent happenings in the past.

In the nineteenth century local antiquarians, particularly Jervise had suggested that there might once have been a camp in the Montrose area. Roman itineraries (written road directories) refer to a place of uncertain location as '*Aesica*'. They posited that this name was a forerunner of 'Esk' and should therefore be located close to either the North or South Esk near their confluences with the sea. But no traces of a military camp that was identified as Roman survived in the area. At this stage few forts had been identified, but one did survive in part as an earthwork at Stracathro. In standard histories this fort was considered of more note for its later medieval history and with so very little other evidence, interest in the subject largely died out.

After the Second World War a new form of analysis – aerial photography – found its way into the archaeological research repertoire and this has allowed the radical revision of the understanding of the presence and survival of archaeological sites across Britain. This 'spy in the sky' has allowed huge areas to be rapidly checked for sites without the need (or cost) of fieldwork, or indeed the need for negotiating access with landowners. Buried archaeological sites affect crop growth above them. If a photographer is available in the right area, at the critical time of crop growth and ripening, then sites can be clearly identified. Generally only larger features – such as major ditches – are visible in this way. Set against this restriction, some site types are so distinctive that they can be identified from photographs alone and do not need subsequent research – such as excavation for example – to confirm their function.

Roman military camps and forts are a case in point. They are ditched enclosures, generally described as 'playing-card shape' – that is rectangular with rounded corners. Entrances are normally visible in each longer side. If a camp is 'temporary' then there will normally be only one surrounding ditch; if it is more permanent then possibly a further one or two might be dug for stronger defence. Occasionally, generally in the more permanent forts, approach or internal roads may also be visible, as are buildings such as barracks, stables, headquarters, or bath houses.

Military rules, regulations, procedures and even buildings and defences, seem to have been the same empire-wide. So military forts and camps, although subject to evolution over the centuries, were extremely similar. It seems that Roman soldiers when on duty always lived within in a camp or fort. There would be (semi-)permanent forts for military units when they were in quarters; but even when they were on campaign they were required to build temporary camps (to the standard design) at the end of every day of a campaign.

Understanding this was a boon to archaeologists involved in aerial photographic research. An army infantry unit could march between 12 and 15 miles each campaign day. If researchers knew where one fort or camp was – for example at Stracathro – then all they had to do was fly a range of 12 to 15 miles and search out the suitable sites for the next. It also rapidly became clear that although the camps were of standard design they were not of standard size. This might depend on the size of the army on the march and the combination of legionary and auxiliary troops, or the balance of cavalry to infantry. However, the size of the camps in the series for each campaign should be the same, so it becomes possible to track the army through its individual campaigns. If one camp is excavated to give a date for the campaign, then that date should hold true for all the similar camps on the route.

Gradually more and more areas of Britain were examined for traces of camps and forts and campaign routes were worked out and dated. However, from this, it seemed that the Roman army in its first-century AD campaign did not pass close to the east coast. Instead it used a route further inland and closer to the higher land, where it would be easier to leave camps to watch or block up movement from the glens. Fortunately Keith St Joseph did not just restrict himself closely to these known routes. In the early 1970s he also checked the Montrose Basin area and there he finally found a small military-type camp at Dun. This camp was smaller than most identified at that stage, but it was single ditched implying that it could be temporary in nature. As a one-off, it could not be dated to any of the known Roman campaigns from aerial photography alone. Confirmation of its date and that it was definitely Roman needed to be made from other forms of research. Shortly after it was discovered it was trial trenched. One sherd of pottery was recovered dating to the late-first century AD. But it was a fine ware and pieces of this type can occasionally survive for many decades if not centuries before breakage and deposition as rubbish, so it could still not be used to securely and closely date the camp.

As the camp lies beside the main Brechin Road and because houses lie within it, there will inevitably be disturbance to the buried archaeological deposits on occasions. One such occasion was when a new gas supply was provided to the cottages in 1990. An archaeologist examined the trenches dug to lay the pipes (which cut across the camp ditches). The presence of the ditches was confirmed. They were the classic V shape of Roman military type together with an 'ankle breaker' trench in the bottom. They had not been re-cut, meaning they represented one short phase of activity. Furthermore, they had not silted up naturally, but had been deliberately been back-filled, implying that the camp had been decommissioned or destroyed not very long after establishment.

Evidence by Tacitus

So what does all this mean in local or regional terms? Who were these Romans, what were they doing here and what effect did they have on the area and people? The Romans were a literate society and documents and other written material survive, covering a range of their beliefs, activities and history. But – and this is a big but – we do not have any native literature

dating to the first century AD. What is the Roman evidence and can we trust the represent-
atives of a hostile state to depict accurately what north-east Scotland was like in this period,
even if they had the inclination to do so.

Ironically, one of the classic Roman texts that survives to this day is the *Agricola* by the
Roman historian Tacitus. This short volume is not a history as we know it but a 'eulogium'.
It purports to narrate the military career of Agricola from his time as a military tribune in Britain
in AD61 to his death in AD93. Critically to our chapter here, he was military commander
in Britain from *c*AD78–84, when he was responsible for the campaigns of invasion that extended
into the north of Scotland. So we need to consider this text to understand what exactly was
going on before, during and after the invasion.

It is important to say at this stage that the document is political, as not only is Tacitus the
son-in-law of Agricola, but the account was written some time after the events. Tacitus had
probably never visited Britain, let alone Scotland, and may have had little opportunity to
discuss the campaigns in detail with his father-in-law. The account is undoubtedly partisan
towards Agricola, who had fallen out of political favour. As Tacitus was also trying to build
himself a political career in the Empire, he needed to support his family's military reputation.
In addition there was never the slightest chance of him questioning the ethics of Roman military
expansion – Rome was right in all things. Not only is he biased, but evidence available from
other sources such as recent archaeological excavations, actually reveals that Tacitus's story
gives substantial distortions of Agricola's activities.

However it gives the broad political and military background to what exactly is going on
at this stage and probably points to why the camp was placed beside the Montrose Basin, and
what the likely outcome was for the local people.

23 *Roman soldier*

AGRICOLA'S CAMPAIGNS

Agricola according to this text was a rising military officer, probably from a provincial family in what is now southern France. We are told he held his first military post in about AD61, as a tribune or junior officer, in the province of Britannia, which at that stage covered southern England and more tenuously parts of Wales. Britannia at this stage was a front line province, still in process of gradual conquest. It had a large standing army of four legions together with auxiliary brigades – numbering between 35,000 and 50,000 troops, whose commanders were directly appointed by the emperor. AD61 was the year of the Boudiccan uprising, when several native tribes had combined to try to eject the Roman occupiers. Roman settlements had been burnt and veterans killed. Much of Agricola's time as an apprentice officer with the army would thus have involved no-holds-barred action as it dealt with all armed resistance, and carried out a process of 'pacification' – stamping out all risks to the army and then keeping firm hold on the area until things had settled once more. After posts in Asia Minor and Rome, Agricola returned to Britain and was put in charge of the 20th legion, pacifying Wales and taking over more of northern England. He moved temporarily to Aquitania, was made a Roman Consul and then returned to Britain in AD78 as a senior commander.

Appointing a loyal officer with good links with the legions in Britain, may have seemed a good idea at the time. Agricola was ambitious and inclined to military activity and the emperor may have come to regret his choice, but surely not more than the 'Caledonians' who ultimately had to bear the brunt of his ambition.

CALEDONIAN DEFEAT – BUT THE ROMANS RETREAT

We are then told that in the seven military seasons Agricola spent in Britain he carried out seven campaigns. In the first he moved into north Wales, in the second he took over northern England, in the third he travelled up the east coast as far as the Tay and in the fourth season he consolidated his position as far as the Forth-Clyde line by building forts. Normally his command would have ended here, but it was extended for a further three years, which he again spent in Scottish campaigns. In his next season he invaded up the west coast of Scotland and contemplated taking Ireland. In his next season he invaded up the east coast – he moved north of the Tay, using a combined army and naval attack. He did not allow his troops into winter quarters but kept them continually in the field. There are hints of problems, for example when the 9th legion was almost defeated and an auxiliary troop deserted. But eventually the main Caledonian army was brought to battle and defeated at '*Mons Graupius*' – probably somewhere in Moray.

But the Roman army then pulled south, took hostages from a tribe called the Boresti (where they over-wintered) and in the spring Agricola left his British command. The security of the German border was deteriorating. A Roman legion had to be withdrawn from Britain and it was impossible for the Romans to consolidate their initial gains. They had to retreat first to the Forth-Clyde line and then back to Hadrian's Wall.

So, if Tacitus's narrative is to be believed, the Roman forces may have been in the general area from AD83 to perhaps AD85. We should be looking for large contingents of the army and the navy as well on occasions. Unfortunately when it comes to checking details, Tacitus is extremely vague on geography throughout his whole text. He does mention the topography, the relationship to the sea and the long summer days of northern Scotland. But he mentions virtually no places by name except for a few of the rivers (which can be conjectured) and the battle site itself, which ironically has still not been definitely located. He refers to the natives as 'Caledonians', but does acknowledge elsewhere that Britain is made up of a number of individual tribes, few of which he names at all. After all, 'one must remember we are dealing with barbarians', to quote one of his phrases. The lack of such subsequent knowledge in later Roman maps, itineraries, or 'geographias' may indicate the short length of time the Romans spent in the area and the lack of peaceful contacts.

Another campaign was mounted under the emperor Severus in the third century and a camp of this period has been identified at Stracathro, but evidence of this later campaign has not been discovered in Montrose area itself yet. Two invasions then, but no permanent or even semi-permanent, conquest.

At the time of the invasion north of the Forth-Clyde line the results of the recent invasion of southern Scotland would not have been seen as either definitive, or permanent, either by the Romans themselves or the surviving locals. We do not know what the relationship would have been like between the tribes south and north of this line previously. We do not know if the northerners had given support to the southerners during the earlier phases of the invasion. Nor do we know how many of the native troops, or families, shifted north into exile to avoid the Romans.

TACITUS ON TACTICS

Tacitus tells us that the war was pushed forward simultaneously by land and sea, and

> *infantry, cavalry, and marines often meeting in the same camp would mess and make merry together. They boasted, as soldiers will, of their several exploits and adventures and matched the perilous depths of woods and ravines against the hazards of storms and waves, victories on land against the conquest of the ocean.*

All very poetic! The navy was used to reconnoitre the way ahead searching out harbours and was used by Agricola to increase his striking power. This could be achieved by providing supplies by sea thus enabling some of his troops to travel faster and lighter. Or possibly contingents of troops were moved northwards by sea – they would no longer be restricted to their usual advance of twelve to fifteen miles a day. Using this method they would find it easier to outflank a native army that lacked an organised navy and that largely relied on infantry. Infantry that incidentally did not consist of a professional army, but local levies drawn from all men and boys of possible fighting age who were available. Native levies would additionally be worried about the safety of their families and farms – both within striking distance of an increasingly mobile and less predictable Roman army.

In the second year of this campaign we are specifically told that the navy was sent ahead 'to plunder at various points and this spread uncertainty and terror' – all part of a deliberate scorched-earth policy to weaken the native population by wrecking their economy and trying to starve them into submission. We have to wonder if this is what happened in the Montrose area and whether our natural harbour had already been identified and suggested as a landing place for raids inland.

Hardships for Local Communities

One particular tactic of Agricola's that Tacitus describes is keeping his army in the field all winter (no doubt unpopular with the troops). This prevented the local levies from safely disbanding and returning to their farms to harvest what crops might remain, replant and see their families and neighbours. This must have had an increasingly serious impact on the local economies probably causing difficulties and starvation on a wide scale, unless local communities collaborated with the Roman army. To quote the natives' military commander Calgacus – "they create a desolation and call it peace".

Undoubtedly these tactics were designed to force the native people into a pitched battle with the Roman army. The options for the native people were stark – an extremely high risk strategy against the largest professional army in the world, or a longer drawn-out war of attrition with Roman scorched-earth policy opposed by guerrilla tactics. Unfortunately the Romans had extensive experience in both types and their military structures were designed for such eventualities, whereas the local tradition was much more peaceful.

Eventually we are told that the Roman strategy led to the battle of Mons Graupius. In a moving speech attributed to Calgacus we are told that the natives decided they had no further options – 'We have no lands behind us, and even on the sea we are menaced by the fleet'. Tacitus claims that on the day the native army stood at an unbelievable 30,000 men with more flocking to the standard all the time. Unsurprisingly he records a massive Roman victory. Again we hear suspicious figures of 10,000 native dead against a paltry 360 legionaries.

The native army, even if a fraction of the 30,000 recorded must have been drawing men and boys and possibly even women from all over north-east Scotland, so it is possible that local people were included in their ranks. Loss of a third of the army on the day alone implies massive grief and trauma for many communities across Scotland. Tacitus tells us that many locals were so disturbed by the Roman success that they burnt their own farms rather than see them taken by the Romans and even killed their families to prevent them being taken prisoner and sold into slavery – 'an awful silence reigned on every hand; the hills were deserted, houses smoking in the distance, and our scouts did not meet a soul'.

Agricola rapidly withdrew from the area, moving into the lands of the Boresti. Before very much longer, either by choice or as a result of an imperial recall, he left Scotland to return to

Rome and eventual disgrace. The Roman army remained. It is likely that at least one contingent occupied Stracathro fort which seems to have been strengthened. But the Roman expansion proved to be unsustainable in the longer term (probably confirming the exaggeration of Tacitus's tale) and the whole army had to be moved south behind the Forth-Clyde line.

With the Romans gone, a no doubt wary local population could try to rebuild their lives. Homes and other buildings would have to be rebuilt. Crops would have to be urgently replanted and stock replaced if possible. Families would have to try and re-form where possible and the wounded would need time to heal. No doubt the survivors would carry the mental trauma of these years for the rest of their lives, but with time the outer structures of their life could and would be rebuilt. For those in the Montrose Basin area the natural food sources may have been their saviour, probably allowing them to recover much faster than in other poorer areas. But it is likely that in future whenever strange vessels were sighted near the shore their pulses would beat a little faster.

6 John Erskine, Reformer

One man stands out above all others in the religious history of the Basin area. That man is John Erskine, the fifth Laird of Dun, whose name appears time after time in the course of the Reformation, not just locally, but as a player of national importance. Erskine was a soldier, diplomat and reformer who played an important role in the advancement of the Protestant cause, the Reformation and its aftermath.

The name of John Knox may be the one we all think of in respect of the Scottish Reformation but he is one of the main sources of the story of the Reformation. As we might expect, his account glorifies his own part in the proceedings.

By the early years of the fifteenth century the Catholic Church throughout Europe had become greedy and inefficient. Many of its senior figures had little or no knowledge of scripture and were interested only in making money for their own use. At the lower levels, the priests were often ignorant and uneducated, unable to administer the Sacraments to their congregations.

These problems were made worse because the Church had so much influence at every level of society throughout Scotland.

Early Life

John Erskine was born in the year 1509. His family, like many Scottish families of the time, suffered terrible losses at the Battle of Flodden in 1513. In the case of the Erskines, John's grandfather, the fourth Laird, also called John, his great uncle Thomas, his father John, who never succeeded to the title of Laird, and his uncle Alexander all died on one of the blackest days in the history of Scotland.

The old Laird had left a will appointing his wife, Margaret Ruthven and another son, Thomas to be his executors. Thomas appears to have taken his duties seriously and made sure that the young Laird received the best education possible.

Among the tutors appointed were James Stewart of Ryland and Thomas himself. In 1526 Robert Melville of Baldovy, father of Andrew Melville of whom we shall hear more later, was one of his curators. (The terms 'tutor' and 'curator' are legal terms for those responsible for the upbringing of pupils or minors where their parent had died. 'Tutor' does not mean that that person would necessarily have been directly involved in the young person's education.)

An Act of the Scots Parliament passed in 1496 had obliged the barons and freeholders of substance to send their eldest sons from the age of eight or nine to grammar schools until they had perfect Latin. They were then required to spend a further three years on the study of art and law.

There is some doubt as to where young Erskine was educated. According to some accounts he attended the University of Aberdeen but the likelihood is that he went abroad for at least part of his schooling.

In some respects, the maturity of young people was viewed differently in those days and when he was 14 years old the young Laird had married Lady Elizabeth Lindsay, the daughter of the eighth Earl of Crawford.

BLOOD MONEY

When the young Laird was aged twenty he became involved in an argument with a local priest called sir William Froster. (The term sir was a designation for priests at that time.) We do not know what the argument was about but it finished with Froster being killed in the bell tower of the Parish Kirk of Montrose. Some sources describe the death as accidental, but what is certain is that the Erskine family had to pay what was then known as 'blood money' to the dead man's parents. In return, they granted Erskine a Deed of Assythement, a form of written pardon, in February 1530.

There is some doubt as to what happened next. Some sources suggest that the Laird fled abroad and others that he went on a pilgrimage as a penance. In fact, as far as we know, Erskine did not go abroad until 1537, having been granted a licence by James V to travel to France, Italy and 'any others beyond sea' for a period of three years. That may have been when he first came across the ideas of the Reformers. Alternatively, the importance of Montrose as a seaport and its consequent links with mainland Europe meant that it is likely that 'heretical' literature would already have been available locally. The upper classes, merchants and seafarers were all exposed to new ideas from the Continent in their travels. That is probably why, in the east of Scotland at least, the reforming traditions came to the fore initially in burghs such as Montrose and Dundee.

It is unlikely that Erskine ever underwent any sort of cathartic conversion. Probably his ideas on religion changed gradually through time and personal study, reflection and experience.

Even before Erskine left Scotland however another sequence of events occurred in 1534 which may have influenced his thinking. One of his friends was David Stratoun whose father owned Lauriston, a property on the east coast a few miles north of Dun, near the village of St Cyrus in Kincardineshire. David Stratoun partly made his living from catching salmon in the North Sea. The Vicar of Ecclesgrieg, the local parish, demanded one-tenth of the fish that he caught as a teind (Church tax; cf tithe) to the Church. Under the Church Law of the period the priest was within his rights. Young Stratoun appears to have been a particularly headstrong young man, too headstrong for his own good. Stratoun told the priest that if the Prior of St Andrews wanted to collect his teind he could come and do so in the same manner as Stratoun himself. On saying this he ordered every tenth fish caught to be thrown back into the sea.

As a result of his actions Stratoun was accused of contravening the rights of the Church and ordered to appear before the Church authorities to answer for his crime. Stratoun's position was that the Church was too greedy and he would not back down. He was found guilty and, like many others to follow, burnt at the stake.

Stratoun had no reputation as a scholar and it is doubtful that he was anything more than 'resentful' of the Church's grasping ways. It has been suggested that his offence was one of 'simple anti-clericalism,' rather than support for any 'heretical' doctrine, but even that may be overstating Stratoun's beliefs.

GEORGE WISHART

Around this time a young preacher called George Wishart was teaching at the Grammar School of Montrose. Although neither of the two men could have had any idea at that time of how events would turn out both Erskine and Wishart would play leading roles in the future of a reformed Scotland. It is generally believed that Wishart's family came from Pitarrow in the Mearns, an area just north of Angus, so it is likely that they already knew each other.

Wishart is reputed to have taught from the Greek New Testament which was in itself seen as heresy and, as such, punishable by death. In 1538 the inevitable charge of heresy was brought against Wishart and he was forced to flee to England, but neither Montrose nor Erskine had seen or heard the last of George Wishart.

By 1540 Erskine was Provost of Montrose, a post that he would hold until his death. At that time Montrose was an important Burgh and, as Provost, Erskine was a commissioner to the Scottish Parliament. The following year Erskine also became Constable of Montrose which position meant that he was responsible for the defence of the Burgh.

Some time around this period he married a French woman called Barbara de Bearle, his first wife having died in 1538. His new wife was a lady in waiting to Marie (Mary) of Guise, the French wife of James V and whatever Erskine's own beliefs might have been by this time the wedding would certainly have been a Catholic ceremony.

The year 1542 saw Erskine set off for Italy with two companions having been given another licence from the King to go abroad, this time for a period of two years. There had been some change in religious thinking for, in 1543, an Act had been passed giving the people the right to read the Bible in English, Scots or 'the vulgar tongue.' Prior to that the possession or reading of the Bible in English or Scots was seen as a heresy and punishable by burning. Although it became theoretically possible to have and read a Scots Bible no such translation existed.

King James V died in 1542 and was succeeded by his daughter Mary who was then six days old. The Earl of Arran was appointed Governor of Scotland. Erskine returned from Italy after only one year away and that is when he is reputed to have brought back the French scholar, Pierre de Marsilier, to teach Greek at Montrose Grammar School.

The same year George Wishart returned to Montrose and from there he embarked on a preaching tour of Angus, Ayrshire and Lothian, before returning again to Montrose. Wishart's desire to preach was overpowering and, despite the ever-cautious Erskine's advice to the contrary, he would not be dissuaded.

Shortly after his return, Wishart escaped capture, or more likely death, thanks apparently to Divine intervention. He had received a letter, supposedly written by the Laird of Kinnear, asking Wishart to visit him, as he was ill. Wishart set off on foot, accompanied by a number of his supporters. Having left Montrose to walk round the north side of the Basin, they had just crossed the Tayock Burn when Wishart stopped and announced that God had forbidden him to continue on this journey. He returned to Montrose leaving his followers to go on a short distance. As they travelled on they saw a group of armed men lying in wait, presumably for Wishart.

Despite this narrow escape Wishart continued to preach and he was eventually arrested and tried. There was no doubt as to the outcome and he was sentenced to death by burning in 1546. Cardinal Beaton watched the sentence being carried out. Within months, Beaton himself had been murdered by Reformist sympathisers.

But Wishart's preaching and example had inspired his bodyguard, a former Catholic priest called John Knox, to become a preacher of the Reformed faith. After the murder of Beaton Knox joined the Reformers in St Andrews castle. When the castle was taken by the French, Knox was sent as a prisoner to the galleys for two years. On his release he went to England.

English Invaders

With the young Queen unable to rule because of her age the country was ruled by a succession of Regents. From 1554, her French mother, Marie, ruled as Queen-Regent. As a result there was considerable French influence and for a time the Auld Alliance was strengthened.

This relationship with France heightened English concerns and Henry VIII, in an attempt to have the Queen betrothed to his son Edward, embarked on what became known as the 'rough wooing.' In 1547 the English army defeated the Scots at the Battle of Pinkie and the young Queen was taken to an island in the Lake of Monteith for her own safety.

Although Erskine was obviously on the side of the Reformers and the Queen-Regent was a supporter of the Catholic tradition he was, first and foremost, loyal to the Crown, if not to the individual. Erskine's relationship with the Queen-Regent was a complicated one. In 1549 he had signed a Bond of Manrent in her favour. (This type of deed was an agreement between two parties, one normally more powerful than the other, whereby the weaker party gave support to the other in return for protection.) During the years 1548 and 1549 there had also been friendly correspondence between the two.

As a loyal Scot, Erskine fought a number of campaigns against the English, before returning home complaining of ill health.

There was by this time a fear of English invasion, with English ships regularly seen off the Scottish coast. Erskine, as Constable of Montrose, collected together a rag-tag army of sorts, composed mainly of his own retainers and local townsfolk, to defend the Burgh. The English did try to invade the town in 1548 but thanks to Erskine's undoubted military skills, a little bit of luck and a lot of courage they were put to flight following what became known as the Battle of the Links.

It was as part of the defences of the town at that time that Erskine built a fort on the site of what is now the Infirmary. For a long time this was known as Fort Hill or Constable Hill, after Erskine. (The site of this fort and the site of the castle, Castlested, are often confused.)

Violet Jacob, one of the last of the Erskine family, writing in her book *The Lairds of Dun* related that by the mid 1550s 'the Laird of Dun had laid by his sword when the smouldering Reformation, whose flame had been overshadowed by the national danger from England, began to glow anew'.

Glow is hardly the right word. The Reformation was about to set the country on fire and the man who would fan the flames was John Knox.

After his time in England, Knox had gone to Geneva to join the Reformers there, but in 1555 he returned to Scotland. Erskine and Knox met in Edinburgh and, as a result of that meeting, Erskine invited Knox to stay with him at Dun. Knox stayed with Erskine for a month, probably preaching in the auld kirkyard on the Dun estate before the rich and poor of Angus. The original kirk, which would have been too small to hold such a congregation, was replaced in the seventeenth century by a much larger building which, according to the Statistical Accounts, had two lofts and held approximately 400 people. This later kirk was demolished on the orders of Margaret Erskine, Lady Ailsa in the early-nineteenth century and the present Dun kirk built. The remaining part of the seventeenth-century kirk, which was later used as a mausoleum for the Erskine family, survives to this day.

24 *The Auld Kirk of Dun, now a mausoleum*

Erskine and Knox became close friends and partners, with Erskine, because of his education and upbringing, being the stronger of the two in areas such as tact and politics. It was in the areas where Erskine excelled that the often headstrong Knox was weakest. As a result they made a good team.

In 1556 Knox returned to Dun where he dispensed the Sacraments to crowds of people from Angus and the Mearns.

As Knox's reputation grew throughout Scotland so did the concern of the ecclesiastical authorities. In May 1556 Knox was summoned to appear at the Blackfriars church in Edinburgh to answer charges against him. Erskine, together with several other sympathisers, was ready and willing to accompany him but in the end the bishops withdrew the summons.

Erskine seems to have had an amazing amount of influence for someone who was effectively nothing more than a middle class baron. In December 1557 a number of leading noblemen signed the 'First Bond,' which resulted in the formation of the body which became known as the Lords of the Congregation. Despite his status, Erskine was the fourth to sign.

Knox had meantime returned to Geneva to continue his work there and only returned when he received a call signed by many of the foremost Reformers, again including that of his old friend Erskine.

Four Funerals and a Wedding

In December 1557 Erskine found his time taken up, yet again by national, rather than Church affairs. This time he was nominated as one of nine commissioners sent to France to witness the wedding of Mary to the Dauphin, Francis, the French crown prince. His fellow commissioners included Lord Rothes, the Bishop of Orkney (Robert Reid) and Lord James Stuart, the illegitimate brother of the young Queen. Again Erskine seemed to be in illustrious company, far above his station in life.

The trip was anything but uneventful. On the outward journey two of the ships sank and Lord Rothes and the Bishop were lucky to escape death by drowning. Once in France matters got even worse. The commissioners, who had been authorised to negotiate terms regarding the marriage, soon found the French making excessive demands on the Dauphin's right to the Scots throne.

They were presumably relieved to be returning home but the drama was not yet over. On the return journey the Bishop, and Lords Cassellis, Rothes and Fleming all died. There was talk of poison which, given their frosty departure from the French Court, may not have been too far-fetched. Certainly, the death of four of the party would seem to be more than just coincidence.

Erskine returned safely to Scotland where he became ever more involved in the Reformed Church. It was Erskine, as one of the principal spokesmen for the Reformers, who was chosen to petition the Queen-Regent to have the Sacrament and services conducted in the vulgar tongue. The Queen-Regent refused to be swayed but her continued intransigence served only to stiffen the resolve of those behind the petition.

As often happens in those situations another event served to bring matters to a head. In this case, the event was the burning in 1558 of yet another Angus martyr. The 'heretic' this time, was Walter Miln, an 80-year old who was the priest at Lunan, just south of Montrose. The death of a third Angus martyr, particularly of such an age, had the opposite effect on the people, serving only to increase their opposition to the Catholic faith.

A further attempt was made to bring the Queen-Regent round to the idea of accepting the Reformed Church, again without success. The Protestant preachers were summoned by the Queen-Regent to Stirling in May 1559, to answer for refusing to attend Mass. The Reformers gathered at Perth and Knox, who had now returned from Switzerland, joined them. Someone had to negotiate and the man chosen was Erskine, who was sent to meet with the Queen-Regent to see if the situation could be resolved. According to Violet Jacob, Erskine found the Queen-Regent to be evasive and felt that she could not be trusted. Jacob was, as ever, writing of one of her ancestors and therefore tended to view Erskine in a sympathetic light. It may be however that Jacob was taking on board the writings of Knox himself. Although hardly neutral, he described Marie as 'a woman born to dissemble and deceive'. He also described the Laird of Dun as, 'a man of most gentle nature, and most willing to please her (the Queen-Regent) in all things not repugnant to God'. Erskine wrote to the Reformers assembled at Perth, requesting that they remain there, which they did.

Marie saw that the preachers were not to obey her summons and had them all put to the horn – a process of outlawry. Erskine, quickly realised the precariousness of his position and in Knox's words, 'prudently withdrew himself'.

Knox preached the following day at St John's Kirk in Perth and when a priest attempted to celebrate Mass in the same building a riot ensued and considerable damage was done to the church and the town.

THE REFORMATION STRUGGLE

The forces of the Queen-Regent massed in Auchterarder, while the Lords of the Congregation set up defences in the City of Perth, where they awaited the arrival of reinforcements from the west. This time it was the Queen-Regent who sought to negotiate and she sent messengers to ask the Reformers under what terms they would surrender.

The Reformers appointed the Laird of Dun and others to negotiate. Their position was simple and to the point. All they were seeking was freedom to worship as they pleased. With reinforcements to the Protestant cause about to arrive, Marie accepted the terms and promised that French troops would not be involved.

No sooner had agreement been reached than Marie attempted to back out of her side of the bargain. Erskine and the other Protestant leaders took their forces to St Andrews which resulted in riots and destruction of Church property there.

The Queen-Regent and her forces had initially intended to attack but found that the Congregation army had been swelled by reinforcements. Almost inevitably an armistice was declared but this soon proved to be useless. The Protestant forces took Perth and the Queen-Regent was forced to seek refuge in Dunbar Castle.

The forces of the Congregation were particularly un-disciplined and they destroyed the Abbey and Palace of Scone. Such actions resulted in a loss of popularity and the Regent's allies were quick to suggest that the Protestant side intended to have Lord James declared King. The Regent's forces marched on Leith, taking that town and eventually the City of Edinburgh itself.

Eventually agreement was reached between the two sides that the Reformers should be able to worship without hindrance provided they allowed the Catholic religion the same privilege. The agreement was more notional than real and the parties continued to battle for overall supremacy.

The death of the French King, Henry II, at this time meant that Mary Stuart became Queen of France and the prospect of increasing French influence became a real threat. French soldiers landed at Leith and proceeded to fortify the town. Alarmed by this the Congregation retreated to Edinburgh where they passed an Act removing Marie. Almost inevitably Erskine was one of the signatories.

The Reformers' army was not strong enough to withstand the forces of the Queen-Regent and having been soundly defeated they were forced to retreat from Edinburgh to Stirling to re-group.

Unsurprisingly, there was strong feeling in Scotland about the level of French influence and, despite traditional enmities, Protestant England now appeared to be a more sympathetic ally. As a result of this change of allegiance, the Secretary of State, Maitland of Lethington, who had joined up with the Reformers, was dispatched to England to enlist the support of Queen Elizabeth.

On Christmas Day 1559 the Congregation's army was driven from Stirling but the arrival of an English army in Scotland forced Marie to seek refuge in Edinburgh.

Although the fighting continued it was inevitable that some sort of compromise would have to be reached and after the Queen-Regent died the Second Treaty of Edinburgh was agreed between the French and English in July 1560. Under the treaty French forces were to be withdrawn from Scotland and the French recognised Elizabeth Tudor as the rightful Queen of England.

THE REFORMATION

At last the goal of the Reformers was in sight. When the Parliament met in 1560 one of its first tasks was to draw up and ratify a Confession of Faith and deal with papal power. 'The thrie estates of parliament has annullit and declarit all sik actis maid in tymes bipast not agreing with goddis word and now contrair to the confession of oure fayth according to the said word publist in this parliament Tobe of nane avale force nor effect.' With these relatively few words the Parliament consigned the absolute rule of the Catholic Church in Scotland to history.

The first ever General Assembly of what was to become the Church of Scotland met in December 1560. The question of how the Reformed Church was to be administered was pressing. It was decided that the way forward was to elect a Commission consisting of thirty commissioners to assist the new clergy and forty-three others, some of whom were to be eligible to preach and instruct. Erskine himself was elected as one of those eligible to preach and, although he was a layman, he was elected as if he were a minister.

It had also been agreed that the country should be divided into five ecclesiastical dioceses for ease of administration. Each area was to be looked after by a Superintendent, a bishop in all but name. Strict rules were drawn up setting out the duties of the Superintendents. They were required to travel about their areas and were not allowed to stay in one place for longer than twenty days and also to preach at least three times per week, although they were permitted to remain in their homes for a maximum of four months in any year. In addition they were responsible for the building of places of worship. The idea was that they should continue with this work until every Church had the services of a Reformed minister.

The five appointees were; John Spottiswood to Lothian, John Willock to Glasgow and the West, John Carsewell to Argyll and the Isles, John Winram to Fife and, inevitably, John Erskine to Angus and the Mearns. The future of the new Church was effectively now in the hands of the five Johns.

The Superintendents themselves were as Violet Jacob put it, 'subject to the correction of elders and ministers of the whole province'.

In 1561 the draft Book of Discipline was considered by Parliament amidst great discussions on the future of Church property. Although the Book of Discipline included fine ideas on education as well as religious matters it was never properly implemented.

Following the death of Francis II in December 1560, Queen Mary, a widow of nineteen, finally returned to Scotland in August 1561. The day after her return she attended Mass, a course of action which did nothing to endear her to the Lords of the Congregation.

When Erskine was installed as Superintendent of Angus and the Mearns, Knox was one those in attendance. Nonetheless Erskine soon found the combination of the workload and being responsible to others brought with it its own problems. At the General Assembly of 1562 Erskine found himself facing allegations that he was admitting priests from popish backgrounds to the Reformed ministry and without submitting candidates to proper examination. It was also alleged that some of the ministers in his area were not fulfilling their duties to their congregation by arriving late for worship and leaving early, afterwards. Presumably the difficulties lay with the shortage of finding suitable candidates for the ministry and, given those shortages, the number of churches for which each minister was then responsible.

The allegations against Erskine appeared to have no effect on his standing in the Church, for, by December 1564, he had been elected as Moderator of the General Assembly. Being elected Moderator added to Erskine's responsibilities and he found himself travelling the length and breadth of Scotland.

Violet Jacob suggested that Erskine had been acceptable to the Queen-Regent as an envoy otherwise he would not have been selected by the Congregation to represent them in their negotiations. This appears to be another of Erskine's attributes. He appears to have been a man who was respected by those who might have seen themselves as his enemy. So it proved with Mary Stuart herself.

When the young Queen wished to hear about the new religion it was Erskine that she asked to hear. She is reputed to have said, "of all others I would gladly hear the Superintendent of Angus, for he is a mild and sweet natured man with true honesty and uprightness".

25 *The meeting of Knox and Erskine with the Queen*

JOHN KNOX AND THE QUEEN

Knox to a large extent was just as he is painted today, forbidding and loud, in its most literal sense. When it appeared that Mary was to marry Lord Darnley, who was a Catholic, Knox made his feelings on the matter widely known, and he was ordered to appear before the Queen at Holyrood to explain himself.

When Knox had his audience with the Queen he was accompanied by his friend John Erskine. According to all accounts of the meeting Knox made his point of view perfectly clear, reducing Mary to tears. It was at this juncture that Erskine is reputed to have told Mary that she was a beautiful woman and that all the princes of Europe would be glad to seek her favours.

Even today Erskine's remarks have been described as fawning flattery. The reason for Erskine trying to calm matters had probably more to do with practicalities than mere flattery.

It is far more likely that Erskine's mild nature, coupled, no doubt, with his sense of survival would have led him to make these conciliatory remarks. Remember too, that as Mary herself was to find out, losing one's head in those days could mean just that. Erskine would have probably have agreed generally with Knox's sentiments, but not with the way he had spoken. He would have quickly realised that Knox had overreached himself and that some attempt had to be made to calm the situation.

Knox was dismissed from the Royal presence but Erskine stayed for a further hour.

THE REFORMATION TAKES ITS COURSE

A measure of Erskine's importance to the Reformation can be seen from the fact that in 1565 and the two subsequent years he was re-elected Moderator of the General Assembly. The account of his appointment refers to him as 'John Erskine of Dun, Knight, Superintendent of Mearns and Angus. From this we can deduce that Erskine had been knighted and this is confirmed by subsequent, but infrequent, references to Sir John Erskine.

Yet again however Erskine faced accusations from his colleagues, this time that he had not carried out the visits to enough kirks during the previous few months. Erskine's reply was that he had been where he was most needed.

Around this time Erskine's health started to fail and he applied to be relieved of his position as Superintendent. His request was refused and a similar appeal the following year met with the same response. Although by this time Erskine would have been in his late fifties we have to remember that we are dealing with the second half of the sixteenth century, when life expectancy was much shorter than today.

But Erskine was in demand to play a variety of roles and his workload appears to have increased rather than decreased.

Erskine served regularly on the Scottish Parliament's committees. In 1564 he had been appointed to serve on a commission to look at the teaching at St Andrews and in 1567 another commission, this time 'anent the jurisdiction of the Kirk'.

Meantime, Mary had been deposed and in July 1567 Erskine, along with the Superintendent of Lothian and assisted by the Bishop of Orkney (Adam Bothwell), crowned the infant James VI as King of Scots. With Mary now a prisoner in Loch Leven castle her half-brother Lord James Stuart, now Earl of Moray, was appointed Regent.

On 20 December 1567 Parliament again ratified the Protestant religion and abolished Papal authority and the Mass.

Around this time Erskine was appointed to serve as a Privy Councillor.

Erskine was also appointed to examine the Universities in the Sheriffdom of Aberdeen and Banff for popery. As a result of his findings the Principal and the Regent of the College of Old Aberdeen were removed from their positions.

The year 1568 saw Erskine in yet another role when he was appointed to a commission to try witches in Arbroath. While this does not fit in with the overall picture we have today of

Erskine, it is likely that he would have seen such an appointment as part of his duty. In any case there does not appear to be any major persecution of witches in Arbroath around that time.

Moray's time as Regent was short lived for he was assassinated on 23 January 1570. According to Woodrow, one of the early chroniclers of Erskine's life, Erskine foretold this tragedy. Moray was staying at Dun and while they were talking Erskine turned to the Regent and said "Ah woe is me, my lord, for what I perceive is to befall you shortly, for in a fortnight's time you will be murdered!" Moray was shot and mortally wounded by James Hamilton at Bothwellhaugh within a month of this conversation.

Money and Power

With the death of Moray a power struggle ensued. The Earl of Lennox became Regent but he was killed in a skirmish and was succeeded by John Erskine, Earl of Mar. (another branch of the Erskine family, not to be confused with the fifth Laird of Dun). There were suspicions however that Douglas, Earl of Morton was the power, if not behind the throne, certainly behind the new Regent.

Parliament had levied a tax of one-third on all Church property, with half of the income going to the Crown and the other half to the ministers themselves. This tax was known as the 'thirds' for obvious reasons. Mar sought to have the funds for himself, although most of the Reformers suspected the hand of Morton behind the scheme. Attempts too were made to restore bishops to the new order, although this was also to regain control of church properties and money.

Erskine wrote to the Regent Mar insisting that the Kirk should have total power in its own sphere. The letter was quickly followed by a second which raised the matter of the thirds, as well as other concerns.

There was to be a conference at Leith to discus Kirk matters and Erskine ended his second letter by stating that there was no point in him, or his colleagues, attending if no discussion about the thirds is to be allowed.

Mar's reply took the wind out of Erskine's sails, regretting Erskine's position and agreeing effectively to restore the status quo.

In 1572 the Conference duly met at Leith. As Mar had withdrawn the offending proposal Erskine attended and appears to have been the spokesman for all the Superintendents. The object of the meeting was to promote better Church government and it had the effect of a General Assembly. Power appears to have been passed to Erskine, Winram and others to look at various matters.

Among the results of the Conference was the re-introduction, at least during the King's minority, of the former style of hierarchy which the First Book of Discipline had abolished. Although the powers of the restored bishops and other officials were greatly reduced this was the start of a long and bitter struggle between the Presbyterian and Episcopalian styles of Church government.

A General Assembly was held in the Tolbooth at Perth with Erskine as Moderator. The decisions previously made at Leith were reluctantly allowed to stand. According to Woodrow, one of Erskine's biographers, Erskine strongly opposed the concept of bishops and consented to the resurrection of the office only to keep the peace. Other, later writers, have suggested that Erskine was a strong proponent of the idea of bishops and the Episcopalian structure. Both sides may have merit in their respective positions since, generally, Erskine appears to have been one for compromise.

Meantime Knox's health was failing and he finally died in November 1572, a few days after Mar. Erskine's second wife Barbara also died during the year.

ANOTHER COMPLAINT

Erskine was the subject of yet another complaint and he had to defend himself yet again before the Assembly. He was charged with having the Kirk on Inchbrayock demolished and having it amalgamated with another. According to Woodrow, Erskine responded "Hearing in my absence that a complaint was given upon me alleging that I had destroyed ... the kirk of Inchbrayock and joining it to the kirk at Maritoun, I ... declare to your wisdoms my part in that cause. I never did destroy a parish kirk but would have the reparation of all. As to that kirk ... I, in my visitation, finding it spoiled and broken, did request that the parishouners repair to the kirk of Maritoun, being near them, until their own kirk was bigged, the which I wish to be done shortly and what is in me lyeth to further the same shall not be omitted. This is the truth ... and if it be found otherwise I shall build the kirk at my own expenses. If your wisdoms think any fault herein, I am subdued, and shal obey your godly judgement."

Violet Jacob reported, 'Their wisdomes had nothing to say'.

The Earl of Morton succeeded Mar as Regent. He had a reputation for greed and he resolved to collect the kirk's monies, proposing that he would collect the thirds rather than those appointed by the superintendents. The result was the extreme shortage of money reaching the kirks and particularly the ministers. Erskine again resigned in protest but again his resignation was rejected and he, together with the other Superintendents who had all followed his example, were requested to stay in office until the next assembly. Erskine was selected to negotiate with the Regent.

In 1575, the Assembly, despite its enthusiasm for his remaining in office, heard yet another complaint against the Superintendent of Angus and Mearns. This time the allegation was that Erskine had admitted an unsuitable candidate to the ministry in Aberdeen. Erskine's response was that the brethren in Aberdeen had approved the appointment. On 11 August 1575 he was presented as the minister at Dun and collated by Winram on the 20th. He resigned his position as minister at Dun early in 1583.

There is no clear evidence as to when Erskine actually resigned from his post as Superintendent, if indeed he ever managed to do so, the post being thought of as being for life.

At the next General Assembly it was decided to appoint visitors to relieve Superintendents of some of their burden and Erskine and his younger son John helped to choose these men who would continue in office until the 'erection' of the Presbyteries.

The Kirk set to work on the Second Book of Discipline and Erskine was employed in its revision and the report put before the Assembly in October 1577. In June of the following year Erskine and his colleagues reported that their deliberations had been put before the King and that he had read it graciously and promised to stand by the Protestant faith.

Erskine continued to have a full workload as a Parliamentary Commissioner and he was appointed to various committees during the late 1570s 'Anent the policy or jurisdiction of the Kirk'. In 1579 he was appointed to a committee to look at the religious views of the 'universitie of S'androis' which was suspected of having popish sympathies.

Morton's dwindling popularity resulted in his complete loss of power by 1580. The young King tried to rule himself but without the strong hand of Morton the country started to deteriorate.

With the country in disarray the General Assembly wrote to the King, and a commission, headed by Erskine, approached the King with a long list of requests.

It was desired that parents be forbidden to send their sons (no equality then) to Paris or other popish places; that 'ordour should be put to Jesuits throughout the country' (the Pestilent Dregs of a most Detestable Idolatory) as the Assembly called them; that nothing should be allowed to interfere with the Assemblies; that excommunication, when pronounced, should be effectively carried out; that another minister should be added to the kings household. According to Violet Jacob the path of all of these ideas was smoothed by the diplomacy of Erskine.

Soon after, Episcopacy again fell from grace and the bishops were ordered to demit their Sees. The Assembly held in April 1581 established Presbyteries as the new method of Kirk government.

THE FINAL YEARS

Erskine appeared by now to be in failing health for he had a licence from the King to eat flesh during Lent and another to permit him to eat meat on the forbidden days of the week.

Meantime the King was determined to re-introduce bishops as he felt that they would strengthen his power over the Kirk.

After the Assembly of 1582 a conference was held between the Assembly Commissioners and those of the Court. This resulted in the King seeking a list of the ministers' grievances. Erskine was among the body that brought their concerns to the King. The complaint was quite straightforward, declaring that the King, urged on by his advisers, was interfering in areas which were the responsibility of the Kirk alone. The King's chief advisers, the Earls of Lennox and Arran were furious and demanded that those present sign what they saw as a 'treasonable document'. Erskine and his associates were aware that signing the deed might be construed as treason and therefore punishable by death. Despite this, they all signed and were allowed to go.

Lennox had already made many enemies in Scotland and he planned to organise a coup, with the intention of re-introducing papacy. Others had different ideas and the King was effectively kidnapped in what became known as the Raid of Ruthven. Erskine appeared as part of a deputation to try to resolve matters, but without success. The King was eventually released having been held 'prisoner' for a period of ten months.

In February of 1587 James commissioned 'Johne Erskyn, Provost of the burgh of montross' and others, to deal with plague 'of the greit witchcraft' in the burgh and surrounding area. Whatever Erskine's views may have previously been on the matter he was now in his late seventies and surely unable to play any active part in rooting out 'witchcraft, necromancie or sorcerie.' Probably this is why William Ramsay and Andrew Beattie, a local Baillie, were also named, with Erskine only mentioned as a courtesy, given his position as Provost.

Later in 1587 Erskine wrote to the King, reminding him of his service, both to James and to his mother, and seeking payment of monies due to him. The King granted for life of those payments he had demanded, in consideration of his; 'long, ernest and fruitfull travellis ... in the suppressing of superstitoune, papistrie and idolatrie'. Violet Jacob describes this as having the merit of a cheap gift, presumably because Erskine was nearing the end of his earthly toils.

By this time William Christison had been appointed to deputise for Erskine and was effectively acting on his behalf in most Kirk matters. The same year saw Erskine make his final appearance at a General Assembly where he was appointed to a committee to collect all the Acts of Parliament concerning the Reformation. The last reference to him in the proceedings of the Scot's Parliament also dates from that year when it relates that all of those on a particular committee had passed away other than Erskine and one other commissioner!

Finally in 1589 he was released from his duties by death.

That is not quite the end of our story for the changes in the Church come, literally, full circle to the town of Montrose.

The General Assembly met in Montrose in the year 1600. As well as the Commissioners James VI was also present, hoping to 'persuade' the Assembly that the Kirk should have bishops.

The King had hoped that at least one of the Reformers would not attend, namely Andrew Melville, of Baldovie. Melville was a renowned scholar, fluent in Greek because of his education and one of the foremost thinkers of the new generation of Reformers.

Andrew Melville was however in the Burgh and his very presence helped to encourage the Commissioners to defy James. With Melville unable to attend the Assembly itself however, the King got his way for the time being.

A Place in History

But what of the position of John Erskine in the Reformation? The status of John Knox as an important figure comes largely from his own account of the Reformation. As a result we can perhaps treat his claims with a certain degree of scepticism.

Knox was a former priest, and as such, he did not have the personal standing to take the noble families of Scotland along with him in his quest for a Reformed Kirk. Certainly no Reformation could have taken place at that time purely from the grass roots. The noble families of the day would have 'strangled' it at birth, if for no other reason than that 'people power' was not to be encouraged.

Was Knox perhaps seen as expendable? He was a useful figurehead and was certainly a strong preacher, but he lacked many of the qualities, such as political awareness, tact and diplomacy, qualities that Erskine seemed to possess in abundance.

While Knox spent a considerable part of his life either in Geneva or England, Erskine seemed always to be at the forefront of the Reformation, consulting with one leader, negotiating with another and seeing to the paper work, as well as dealing with Parliament and the General Assembly. Erskine appears to have had people skills. He was certainly respected by all of his peers, including, it would appear, many of those who did not share his views. As well as being the person chosen to negotiate on behalf of the Reformers he was often chosen to arbitrate in civil disputes.

Erskine deserves to be recognised as one of the major players in the history of the Reformation.

26 *Erskine family crest*

7 West Indian Fortunes at Langley Park

First Known as Ecclesjohn

One night in January 1787 at Ecclesjohn, the mansion house we know today as Langley Park, a man lay screaming and rolling in pain on the floor, his head cradled by his frightened wife. The man was James Scott, the fourth laird of the Scott family to own the estate of Ecclesjohn which lay between Dun and Tayock on the north side of the Montrose Basin. James Scott's unfortunate condition was due to the immoderate consumption of spirits, often laced with opiates. By his own admission to the clergyman who attended him, he habitually drank two quantities of raw spirit even before breakfast. His alcoholism together with his own and inherited debts brought to a sad conclusion 63 years of otherwise respectable Scott lairds at Ecclesjohn.

Originally an early-medieval parish first appearing in records in the fourteenth century, Ecclesjohn belonged to the Barony of Dun and to its feudal lords, the Erskines of Dun. After 1409, the Erskines renounced the overlordship to the powerful Bishopric of Brechin and for the next two centuries, the Erskines of Dun became, in effect, the Bishops' hereditary tenants. This state of affairs continued until 1615 when the estate passed to a satellite branch of the family, the Erskines of Kirkbuddo. By the eighteenth century Ecclesjohn's feudal ties were finally severed when prosperous local merchants from Montrose, first the Milnes and then the Scotts snapped up this pleasant local estate with its glorious views across the Basin. When Colonel James Scott bought it in 1726, 'the lands of Eaglesjohn' included 'a mansion with gardens, orchards, fishponds, doocots and woods'. The kirk was long since derelict and the parish had been absorbed into neighbouring Dun.

THE JAMAICAN CONNECTION

The Scotts, a prolific landowning dynasty around the Montrose area, had made their fortune by specialising in the export of locally caught salmon. George Ogilvy of Langley, Jamaica, who bought Ecclesjohn from the alcoholic James Scott in 1787, had made his money overseas. He was a member of the new breed of super-rich investors who were buying up properties all over Britain and embellishing them with new money derived from British overseas possessions, either from the East Indian Company or, as in the case of George Ogilvy, from their West Indian sugar estates. Already on the other side of the Basin, Hercules Ross, another West Indian magnate had bought the estate of Craig and was busy drawing up plans to build Rossie Castle. At nearby Rosemount, John Duncan would soon build a fine mansion with money from the East Indian Company.

Sadly, George Ogilvy's tenure at Ecclesjohn was cut short after four years by his untimely death aged 47 in 1791, but he lived long enough to effect important changes. It was his decision to change the name to Langley Park after his estates in Jamaica. He also enlarged the policies by buying the lands of Tayock in 1790. He and his wife Barbara Dundas ran a sizeable establishment. He paid servants' taxes on a butler, a coachman, a gardener, a cook, a lady's maid, a laundry maid and a chambermaid. No doubt, Ogilvy had hoped to make his mark in local affairs. He had been made a burgess of Montrose in 1786 and he subscribed to the new South Esk Bridge before he died. His gravestone at the Episcopal Church of Montrose bore the inscription, 'George Ogilvy Esq. Late of Langley Park and Tayock, near Montrose and of Langley estate in Jamaica.'

27 *The carriage of Mr and Mrs James Cruikshank arriving at Langley Park*

THE NEW OWNER FROM ST VINCENT

In 1792, a new carriage rolled up the hill to the mansion at Langley Park. The door panel bore a crest featuring an armed hand holding a dagger, the crest of the Cruikshank family, descendants of the ancient family of Asswanley of Banff. Inside the carriage sat Margaret-Helen, the grand-daughter of the very Reverend Alexander Gerard, Doctor of Divinity at Kings College, Aberdeen and her new husband the very rich 44-year old James Cruikshank Esq. of Richmond, St Vincent.

Once again, Langley Park had acquired a West Indian magnate as its new laird. This time, the family fortune had been made in the Windward Island of St Vincent, where James and his younger brothers, Patrick, John and Alexander possessed vast sugar estates. The Cruikshank family channelled their handsome profits into property acquisitions in Angus, thereby founding a new land-owning dynasty in the area. By the time James had bought the Langley Park Estate, the second brother, Patrick was already established at 'Strickcathro' although it was to be his youngest brother, Alexander, who purchased Stracathro from Patrick's heirs in 1820 and who built the fine mansion house that we know today. In 1818 John bought the estate of Keithock on the Edzell side of Brechin.

THE SLAVERY QUESTION

What would the local climate of opinion have been towards these wealthy new landowners whose fortunes were derived from slave labour? The Caribbean sugar plantations absorbed nearly half of all African slaves; such was the need for intensive manpower in the hot and backbreaking conditions in which only slaves would work. For example, on the St David's estate on St Vincent belonging to James's brother Patrick, 347 Negroes toiled on 500 acres of sugar plantation to produce an impressive 723,000 lbs of sugar and 18,140 gallons of rum over two years between 1827 and 1829.

For some time, however, a nationwide revulsion to the practice of slavery had been gaining momentum. As early as 1788, the Montrose Town Council had joined in, instructing their Member of Parliament to support the abolition of slavery in Parliament. In 1792, the very year in which James Cruikshank bought Langley Park, the Council unanimously agreed to petition Parliament to 'abolish a commerce so disgraceful to a free and enlightened nation'.

In reality, the fulminations of the Council did not sit well with the earlier involvement of the town magistrates in the slave trade. Many of them had made large personal profits from trading in tobacco, itself farmed with slave labour and imported in the same ships that carried slaves from Africa to the plantations. The odds are that the pragmatic local mercantile community managed to swallow their scruples. Without doubt, they would have admired the tenacious entrepreneurship of the rich sugar planters who were, after all, legends of their time. There was also money to be made from the planters' generous patronage of local businesses. Their profits, which they ploughed into the local economy continued to be vast as the period of the Anglo-French Wars from 1793 to 1802 and 1803 to 1815, were prosperous times for the West Indian magnates with sugar commanding record prices. There was no shortage of money at Langley Park to fuel a lavish lifestyle. By the time slavery was finally abolished in the British colonies in 1833, the Cruikshanks and their fellow planters were well established in local society.

THE NEW BUILDING PROGRAMME

All the signs are that James and Margaret-Helen Cruikshank settled down very quickly to the life of landed gentry at Langley Park. Within a short time they launched into an ambitious building programme, beginning with a substantial new stable block in the newly favoured battlement style, a very grand affair built around a large arena with unusual curved stone walls within which horses could be schooled. The Cruikshanks were keen on their horses, both for transport as carriage and saddle horses, and for sport at hunting and racing.

On the southwest drive two new lodges were built, one with new gates on the Brechin to Montrose toll road, and the other half way up. The mansion too was remodelled. In 1797,

28 *Langley Park House c1910. (Crown Copyright: RCAHMS)*

James Cruikshank had acquired a substantial square three-storey house, of seven windows width across both the front and sides. To this he added an imposing porch, supported by four fluted columns. He had large bow windows thrown out on the ground and first floors to the Basin side of the porch and enlarged some of the windows on the southern side, thus opening up from the house the superb view across the Basin especially from the first floor, the 'Piano nobile', where the drawing room and other important public rooms would have been situated.

These rooms would also have made an ideal base for one of James Cruikshank's favourite hobbies for he was a keen amateur astronomer. The view of the night sky over the Basin would have been unparalleled. Perhaps he invited fellow astronomer, James Norval, to share his telescope. Norval was a schoolmaster in Montrose, who gave a series of lectures on astronomy, later published in a book called *Popular Lectures on the Solar System and Fixed Stars*.

In the 1820s, James Paterson, a local artist produced a series of views from gentlemen's seats including Langley Park. The accompanying description reads:

> *Langley Park, the delightful residence of James Cruickshank, Esq. – than which there is hardly to be found a situation commanding a more varied and interesting prospect. Langley Park is a very fine building, surrounded with large trees and the gardens and walks are laid out in a most tasteful and elegant manner, so as to increase, in a high degree, the richness of the scene.*

That scene shows a superb vista stretching down beyond the wooded slopes of the estate to the basin at high tide, with the masts of the ships in the harbour, the town and beyond it the open sea and still more shipping.

Fine Gardens

The same view could be seen from the elegant formal gardens to the east of the mansion which comprised not one, but three walled-gardens which must have been some of the finest in the area. Much later, in 1899, the still fine gardens were reproduced as a postcard showing well stocked flowerbeds and rose arches through which Montrose and its distinctive steeple can be seen. The sheltered vegetable beds and extensive glasshouses would have furnished the Cruikshank household with abundant everyday vegetables and fruit as well as the more exotic plants and fruits that were fashionable at the time. It seems that the gardens were well known as, in May 1819, *The Montrose Review* reported that:

> *Amongst the early productions of this remarkably prolific and congenial season, it may be worthy of note that Mr Cruikshank of Langley Park ... had artichokes, cherries and new potatoes last week, the produce of his own garden.*

In the same year, peaches and plums from Langley Park were pronounced the best in the show at the quarterly meeting of the Montrose Florist Society. Horticultural successes continued over the years. Langley Park's produce regularly won awards, including its morello cherries and melons and 'a brace of large cucumbers' one of which was 17 inches long!

29 *Postcard of Langley Park Garden 1899. (Crown Copyright: RCAHMS)*

As Painted by Raeburn

No country gentleman's house was complete without family portraits. James Cruikshank was rich enough to employ one of the top portrait painters of the time, so he and Margaret-Helen sat in Edinburgh for Henry Raeburn. Today, these portraits hang in the Frick Gallery in New York. They are believed to have been painted between 1805 and 1808 when James Cruikshank would have been in his late fifties. He looks very young for his years, confident, with a slight swagger in his manner of sitting. He is fashionably dressed with a double-breasted grey coat with brass buttons, knee breeches and white stockings. The buttons are rather strained, perhaps a tribute to the good table kept at Langley Park! His grey hair is curled in the new style without wig or powder and he has slightly ruddy cheeks, a result perhaps of having lived in the tropics. His wife looks younger than him, a pretty, plumpish woman with dark hair and the hint of a smile as permitted of the time. Her clothes look expensive – a fur-trimmed rich brown velvet coat worn over a ruffle-collared cream dress. The matching velvet hat she holds in her lap is trimmed with a grey ostrich feather.

Margaret-Helen bore James Cruikshank six children. In 1798 the twins James, the future heir, and his sister, Elizabeth, were born. Patrick followed in 1800 and then three more daughters: Clementina, Margaret-Helen and Mary.

The Landed Gentleman

While Margaret-Helen busied herself bringing up the children, James looked to the future of his estate. In 1815, he acquired from Hedderwick the lands of Brucemill and Glenskinno. Later, he gave Glenskinno to his second son who styled himself Patrick of Glenskinno. In 1819 James also bought the lands and the mill of Newbigging. These land acquisitions would appear to have been a shrewd investment. In August 1819 *The Montrose Review* reported that

> *The present abundance of money in the country and consequent low rate of interest has raised the price of landed property in Scotland so lately depressed. Demand for landed property is daily increasing.*

Now in his mid-sixties, James continued to lead the life of a respectable country landowner. In 1814 he joined other gentlemen of the county of Forfarshire and Kincardineshire including the Hon. William Maule of Panmure, Peter Arkley of Dunninald, and John Duncan of Rosemount in an Association for the preservation of game on their estates. The following year at the Autumn Show of the East Forfarshire Farming Association at Trinity Muir, Brechin, he won three guineas for the best two-year-old pony. He did his bit for local charities too. In 1820, he gave £5 to the Fever Ward on Rossie Island and in the same year he donated a generous £25 towards the newly extended Town House in Montrose. He was a Justice of the Peace and a deputy Lord Lieutenant and was on the board of management of the local Royal Lunatic Infirmary and Dispensary.

30 Mr James Cruikshank *by Raeburn. (Copyright: The Frick Collection, New York)*

THE SON AND HEIR IN FRANCE

On the family front, his chief preoccupation had been the future of his eldest son James. Never one to accept anything but the best, he arranged for his entry into a crack cavalry regiment, the 18th Royal Hussars. This fashionable regiment was one of the most dashing of the Napoleonic Wars. James was commissioned in May 1815 as a cornet, too late to participate at Waterloo but in 1817 he served as a lieutenant in the army of occupation in France. James's time in the 18th Hussars would have been extremely formative both in the acquaintances he made and in learning to be a bit of a 'swell', dressed in the highly embellished and striking blue uniform with sky blue facing, trimmings of lace and the distinctive fur cap head-dress. As was the custom of the regiment he had to sport a moustache. The officers of the army of occupation lived rather well in France – they even kept a pack of hounds. James seems to have interspersed his military duties with amorous adventures in the company of a young Count,

31 Mrs Margaret-Helen Cruikshank *by Raeburn. (Copyright: The Frick Collection, New York)*

the Conte de la Pasteur who set their escapades to verse! The objects of their affection were two sisters, Amanda and Charlotte St Clair. The Count's poem reads:

> *Thus months were passe'd in billing and cooing,*
> *Cruikshank and the Count going courting together,*
> *The pretty St Clairs always a suing,*
> *And out all the night in spite of the weather –*
> *But one thing in view, and that was wooing;*
> *Cruikshank all willing to share his heather,*
> *And Scott's moors with his adored Charlotte,*
> *And dress her in future in tartan and scarlet.*

Despite his devotion, however, James must have changed his mind, because when he left the regiment in 1818 he returned to Montrose without Charlotte!

32 *Hussar*

SETTLING DOWN IN MONTROSE

The signs are that he settled down to local life. He attended the show of the Eastern Forfarshire Farming Association on Trinity Muir in 1819 and afterwards in the town hall at Brechin he was admitted as a new member of the Association by unanimous ballot, a sign he was beginning to take on the responsibilities of his inheritance. For his leisure time, there were new amenities available in Montrose. In October 1819 the newly redecorated Theatre Royal opened. James might have gone to see Mr Ryder's production of 'Othello' or 'Rob Roy Macgregor' with the band of the Forfarshire Militia playing several select airs between the acts. Even more appropriate would have been the musical farce entitled 'Of Age Tomorrow,' as this was James's twenty-first year! In October 1820 the first Montrose Assembly was held in the newly refurbished and spacious Town House, heralding the beginning of the dancing season.

WEDDING BELLS

Perhaps James danced with his bride-to-be in the new Assembly Rooms, for in 1821 he married Lady Anne Letitia Carnegie, daughter of the seventh Earl of Northesk, a naval hero of the recent wars, having been third in command at the Battle of Trafalgar in 1805. Her maternal grandfather, William Henry Ricketts, also had interests in the West Indies. James Cruikshank Senior must have been very satisfied – a titled wife for his heir and possibly an heiress to boot.

1821 must have been a year of great rejoicing at Langley Park as on 12 February another marriage took place in the family between James and Margaret-Helen's youngest daughter Mary, to her cousin Alexander Cruikshank of Keithock. A new generation of Cruikshanks was putting down roots.

Lady Anne and James Junior went on to have a large family, spanning 19 years of childbirth. Their first born, Mary, was delivered at Langley Park in January 1822. After this they moved to Anniston, near Inverkeilor, where their son and heir, James Alexander, was born in March 1823. Two more boys, William and Patrick, followed in 1825 and 1826, then Margaret, a companion for Mary at last, in 1827; finally, four more sons, Edward, Alexander, John and Augustus. In 1841, a last-minute addition to the family appeared in the person of a third girl, Elizabeth.

The End of an Era

The grandchildren must have been a great consolation to the old James Cruikshank after the death of his wife Margaret-Helen, aged 53 in 1823. James himself lived another seven years dying in 1830 at the great age of 82. Clearly possessed of a strong constitution having survived the punishing conditions of the Tropics, he arrived in Montrose a middle-aged man of 44 and went on to enjoy the fruits of his labours until old age. He must have died a contented man. He had built up and embellished a fine estate, raised a large family, successfully launched his eldest son who had made a fine marriage from which a good clutch of heirs had materialised to ensure the succession at Langley Park.

The Fast Set

He may, however, have entertained just a few reservations about his son's lifestyle for all the signs point to the young James Cruikshank belonging to a fast set of racy friends who gambled heavily on their own and their friends' sporting abilities. James Junior was himself a crack shot, an able golfer and an enthusiastic participant in all field and turf sports. Unfortunately, sport of all sorts had become irretrievably tied up with gambling and increasingly no horse could be ridden, no shot fired, nor golf club swung without having a price on its outcome.

To understand James's involvement in this world, we need to look at some of the local friends with whom he grew up. A childhood neighbour down the road at Dun, only four years his senior was Lord Archibald Kennedy, son of the wealthy twelfth Earl of Cassillis and of Margaret Erskine, the second daughter of John Erskine of Dun. The young Lord Kennedy spent a lot of his childhood at Dun under the influence of the sixteenth laird, his aunt Alice, who was horse-mad, owned a pack of harriers, ran her horses in the local Montrose races and was a great gambler. Her nephew would follow in her mould. When only 19, he married a local heiress, Eleanor Allardyce of Dunnottar, near Stonehaven. (Her fortune also derived from West Indian sugar trade profits.) Three days of celebrations marked the wedding at Dun before Kennedy proceeded to storm through Eleanor's fortune with a life of outrageous sporting wagers and gambling in which James was frequently involved.

Another partner-in-crime and neighbouring childhood friend, only three years his junior was Captain Horatio Ross, son of that other West Indian investor and builder of Rossie Castle. The godson and namesake of Admiral Nelson, Captain Ross was an outstanding sportsman, winning large sums in shooting and steeplechasing.

On a famous occasion at a dinner at Dun during race week at Montrose, Lord Kennedy sprung a golfing wager on James. Three holes of golf were to be played that night (it was then about 10pm) in the dark with the only illumination to be lamps placed at each hole and those carried by either player. The stake was an incredible £500 a hole. Each contestant hired boys to listen out for the ball and to find where it landed. Lord Kennedy won by a hole taking the same number of strokes as he had by daylight, despite the night being dark without much moonlight. How to lose the equivalent today of £20,000 in one evening!

James Junior and Lord Kennedy were frequent opponents on the golf course in daylight too. On the St Andrews Links in August 1824 *The Montrose Review* reported that Lord Kennedy challenged James to six matches of 7 holes each, for 50 guineas a match ('besides a number of bets'). The match drew large crowds and this time James emerged victorious by six games to one having received 'considerable odds from his lordship.' According to *The Review*, Kennedy had been more successful in a shooting bet the previous week, challenging James to shoot ten brace of grouse with single balls in one day. This time Kennedy, an outstanding shot, won the contest bringing down twenty birds with 170 shots. It is not reported how much money changed hands.

33 *Golf match*

THE FANCY IN LONDON

James' sporting life was not confined to Montrose. In 1824 he featured in a shooting match at the Red House Tavern in Battersea, London. This was a regular playground for a notorious sporting and gambling club known as the 'Fancy'. Its members bet heavily on sporting fixtures such as boxing and shooting matches. A large crowd of gentry watched James partner Lord Kennedy against his neighbour Captain Horatio Ross and George Osbaldeston, the well known sportsman for 1,000 guineas prize money in a pigeon shooting match which lasted two days. Huge bets were placed but the result was a draw. This event was mentioned in *The Montrose Review* which proudly reported that 'Mr Cruikshank's shooting was the steadiest – and he bagged the greatest number of birds'.

MAGNUMS OF CLARET IN MONTROSE

Back at home in Scotland, there was a gentlemen's club which traded in wagers of a more modest kind. It was called the Montrose Club but the membership included most of the landowners from the surrounding countryside. They met and dined at four in the afternoon on the first Monday of every month at Hunters Inn, Montrose (renamed the Star Inn in 1809). James Cruikshank Senior had been a member and occasionally presided over the meetings. There is no record of him making bets, however, unlike his son who appears to be something of a serial wagerer – though no worse than many of his fellow members! The stake was always the same – a magnum of claret. In June 1823, James bet that the Fife and Forfar Hounds would kill more foxes between 1 October 1823 and 1 May 1824 than the Ayrshire foxhounds. He miscalculated and had to pay the usual damages of one magnum of claret which was meticulously recorded as 'Drunk on June 5th 1825'.

Such bets show James to be a keen huntsman. Others reveal his interest in horse racing and knowledge of the form of runners in national race meetings. In December 1824 he challenged Sir Alexander Ramsay of Balmain to name the winner of next year's Derby and in January 1825, he bet against David Carnegie of Craigo as to the winner of the 'Ledger'. Golfing bets featured too. He challenged Mr Scott at golf in August 1823 and Mr Greenhill of Fearn in 1829 'with an iron and a putter'. Both Mr Scott and Mr Greenhill lost and had to pay up.

One non-sporting bet he made in 1833 concerned the price of sugar in 'West India' when he bet Mr Anderson that the present duty of sugar was 27 shillings. Mr Anderson bet on 24 shillings and won the bet. James Cruikshank Senior must have turned over in his grave. He would have had the up-to-date information at his fingertips, although just how close the connection was between the Cruikshanks and their West Indian lands by 1833 is not known.

DANCING AND DINING

One of the other functions of the Club was to conduct the Assemblies (social gatherings of the local gentry with dining and dancing which took place during the winter months) and to submit annual accounts for them. James's wife Lady Anne was given the honour of presiding over the Assembly in 1827 with Sir Alexander Ramsay of Balmain. With such an active social life, it is small wonder that James had the need of the eighteen pairs of gentlemen's dress gloves (extra large!) which are recorded in the accounts of a Montrose shopkeeper in 1829.

Lady Anne seems to have been as active as James in fashionable county life. In 1820, she appears as co-director with Captain Skene of Careston of a fashionable dining club, 'The Beef Steak Club', which met at the New Inn, Forfar. This club originated in London and included among its membership the Prince Regent and other fashionable wags of Regency London. It was founded as a protest against the current fashion for fancy French food such as *fricassees* and *soupe-maigres*. Instead, vast quantities of 'manly' beef steaks were consumed and were washed down with punch rather than French wines or champagne. James, however, may have found it rather difficult to remain loyal to the Club's principles. He and other members of the Montrose Society had patriotically deprived themselves of French wines during the Napoleonic wars. But once hostilities had ceased, with obvious relief, they declared themselves free from the ban, after complaints about the quality of the wine during the war years!

TURF SPORTS

Other key local social gatherings centred round race meetings. The Montrose Races held on the Links racetrack enjoyed a revival between 1821 and 1826. James's friend Lord Kennedy, who had his own pack of hounds and racehorses at Dunnottar, had regular runners at Montrose and also at Aberdeen. Both James Cruikshank Senior and Junior were devoted race goers. In 1821 the younger James Cruikshank was a steward at the July meeting in Montrose. In 1823 the three Cruikshank ladies – Mrs Cruikshank Senior (who died later that year), Lady Anne, and her sister-in-law from Keithock were among the largest subscribers, contributing three guineas each to the Montrose Ladies Subscription Purse race. In the same year, James Junior entered a runner 'The Devil' in a Pony Match once round the course against Mr Maule's pony 'All Steel' although it is uncertain whether the race was run as no result is recorded.

In addition to flat racing, steeplechasing, although still in its infancy, was already pursued in Forfarshire and James was an active participant. For example, in 1831 *The Sporting Magazine* reported that 'sportsmen mustered strong for a gallant steeplechase' from The Laws, towards Linlathen, finishing at Gagie. Mr Cruikshank's entry was called 'His Worship' ridden by Captain Hunter although unfortunately he was unplaced against the five other runners. In 1833, back at Montrose, James rode his own pony in a race. An ex-cavalryman, he was obviously as at home in the saddle as he was with a gun or a golf club. The race was for £20 a side against Captain Raitt of Anniston who also rode his own pony. Unfortunately, James lost by two lengths. The race was mentioned in *The Montrose Review* which reported that nearly all the gentry in the neighbourhood were present and that the same ponies were to be matched in a steeplechase the next month.

County Duties and Politics

Fortunately, James Cruikshank's life was not all sport and gambling. By 1828 he was a Justice of the Peace and a Deputy Lord Lieutenant having received his commission as a Major in the Forfar and Kincardineshire militia. From now on he is often referred to as Major Cruikshank. In 1831 he would have been busy directing the militia exercises on the Links at Montrose.

In 1830 he began to dabble in local politics when he supported his old friend Horatio Ross who was standing as prospective MP for the Angus burghs against the Tory candidate Sir James Carnegie. James accompanied Ross to various receptions held around the county including one at Arbroath where he gave an eloquent speech in support of his friend and proposed the toast to 'The Commercial Interests of the Angus boroughs'. *The Review* reported that on the way to Brechin, at the Leuchland Toll, the two friends were met by a dense crowd who unyoked the horses and pulled their carriage into the city. Flowers were strewn before them (how many a politician today would covet that sort of welcome!) Unfortunately, Ross was defeated.

In 1831 James again entered the political arena on the occasion of the County elections brought about by the retirement of William Maule, newly created Lord Panmure. This time, freed from the ties of friendship, he changed sides and showed his true political colours. This was a time of furious national debate about parliamentary reform and the extension of the voting franchise, which was to end in the Reform Bill of 1832, championed by among others the Montrose-born Joseph Hume, the Radical politician. Our James Cruikshank, however, positioned himself in the opposing camp, as the great reactionary, championing the anti-reform candidate the Hon. Donald Ogilvy, and speaking out against 'the nefarious (reform) bill'. *The Montrose Review*, on the side of the reformers, showed no mercy, branding James 'the oracle of the Angus Tories'. this 'Solon of the North' who dares to call the wisdom of the ministers 'nefarious'. This time, James backed the winning candidate, but not without some shenanigans at the election meeting when he had to request a delay as several of the freeholders failed to turn up on time, some of whom, according to *The Review*, hailed from Aberdeenshire and had dubious claims to be eligible to vote at all!

In 1832, James was back in favour with *The Review* this time praising his seemingly well known generosity. The occasion was the breaking up of part of the grass parks on the Langley Park home farm to which end his tenants and some local farmers offered him a 'love-darg'. This was in effect a free day's work. James offered a premium 'with his usual liberality' to the best ploughing performance. Afterwards, he gave horses and men substantial refreshment followed by dinner for the judges and the owners of the ploughs at the mansion where the evening was spent 'in that happy way common on such occasions'.

DEBTS HIT HOME

In the same year, however, James's old friend Lord Kennedy died. Moreover, there were signs that James was now paying the price for some of the worst excesses of his earlier lifestyle associated with that gentleman. Financial troubles had hit home. In the year of his father's death in 1830, he had already begun to borrow against the Langley Park estate. He borrowed £8,880 from his cousin Alexander Cruikshank at Keithock, £3,000 from his friend Horatio Ross and resorted to the last resort expedient of raising money, another £8,800, from an insurance company, The North British. Other loans, although for lesser amounts, are also recorded. Finally in 1833 the Trustees appointed by his father obtained an Act of Parliament authorising them 'to sell parts of the Entailed Estate of Langley Park and apply the price thereof to the extinction of debts'. Still James continued to borrow, however, this time £4,000 from the Aberdeen Fire and Life Assurance Company in 1836.

The truth was that in the 1830s many a Scottish laird was in the same boat. Past debts from an extravagant lifestyle encouraged by spectacular rises in rents and land values during the French wars were causing problems to many. Falling rents from farms were compounding the problem. The ploughing up of the grass parks may have been symptomatic of the situation. In addition, James had the care of a very large family. He had to make provision for ten children of whom only one, a son, John, died young. There would be marriage contracts to make, a settlement for Lady Anne should she be widowed and provisions for the younger children. We also do not know if he was still receiving income from the old family estates in the West Indies. Apart from the general difficulty of extracting money from Caribbean assets there was also the knock-on effect of the abolition of slavery in the British Colonies in 1833. Even if the estates were still in his possession, the income from them would have been drastically reduced as wage bills soared with the end of cheap slave labour.

THE SURVIVAL OF THE ESTATE

A combination of events led to James's financial problems, but when he approached middle age and looked back over the extravagances of his earlier life, he may have rued the day that he forgot to abide by the Cruikshank family motto which was '*Cavendo Tutus*' – By Caution, Safe!

He died in 1842 when only 44. His widow was left to struggle with his debts and the bringing up of nine children ranging from Elizabeth aged two to the nineteen-year-old son and heir James Cruikshank the third. He died seven years later when only twenty-six years old and, although married, had no children. The next son, William, was also laird for only seven years and also died young without an heir. These were hard years for the family. Unable to afford to live at Langley Park, they were forced to live an itinerant lifestyle, and found tenants for the mansion whenever they could.

Meanwhile, the family line was further depleted by the premature death of the next three surviving sons, Patrick, Edward and Alexander. The remaining son, Augustus Walter, who as the youngest brother had never expected to inherit, succeeded in 1856 and for a short time managed to move back to Langley Park with his wife and family and a substantial staff, suggesting a revival of the family fortunes. He died aged 81 in 1918. Unlike his older brothers at least he inherited the longevity gene from his grandfather. The last and sixth Cruikshank laird of Langley Park, James Walter, the oldest son of Augustus Walter, lived in America. He sold off parcels of the estate but the mansion, the immediate policies and the home farm although regularly tenanted, remained in the family possession until their sale in 1940, one hundred and forty-eight years after the first James Cruikshank arrived with his West Indian fortune.

34 *Cruikshank family crest*

8   The Pursuit of the Redfish

A History of Salmon Fishing in Montrose Basin

Like a stone dropped in a pool, every major historical event creates ripples. The murder of Thomas à Becket, swiftly followed by his canonisation, led King William the Lion of Scotland to dedicate his newly-founded Abbey at Arbroath to St Thomas in 1178. The Founding Charter of the Abbey included a gift of fishing on the North Esk, part of which, at Warburton, was described as the 'St Thomas Net'. Thus one of the smaller ripples caused by that injudicious murder at Canterbury finally fetched up on the banks of a river on the east coast of Scotland.

This is the first documentary evidence we have for the existence of the organised catching of salmon in the Montrose area. Montrose had, of course, a natural advantage when it came to the catching and exporting of salmon. The North and South Esk and Montrose Basin provided ample supplies of the prey, while the town provided the manpower to trap and net it, the barrels and kits to pack it, and the harbour to export it. The number of species of fish and crustaceans in the Basin is surprisingly varied. They include not only those commercially fished such as salmon (sometimes referred to by superstitious fishermen as the redfish), sea-trout, eels, and mussels, but those which provide the tug of attraction to the angler – salmon and sea-trout again, of course, and brown trout. Less well known inhabitants are pike, perch, and flounder and juvenile forms of sea-fish such as cod, codling, herring, and saithe, making up a total of more than 20 species in all.

Salmon has always been, of course, the main allure of those seeking to make a living, large or small, from the bounty of the Basin and the South Esk. The first mention of fishing rights belonging to Montrose itself is found in the earliest burgh charter of 1369:

> The Charter of David the Second, King of Scots, dated in the fortieth year of his reign, and contained in the register of the Great Seal, grants to the Burgesses and Community of our Burgh of Monros, all our Burgh of Monros, with the fishings within the waters of Northesk and South Esk, in cruives, yairs, and nets of old accustomed usage.'

EARLY FISHING METHODS

These 'cruives, yairs and nets' are the earliest ways of catching salmon for which we have documentary evidence. Being of 'old accustomed usage' in the twelfth and thirteenth centuries implies a venerable history.

Several centuries before that, Bishop Winfrid of Colchester, writing in the time of Bede,

> found so much misery from hunger, he taught the people to get food by fishing. For, although there was plenty of fish in the seas and rivers, the people had no idea about fishing, and caught

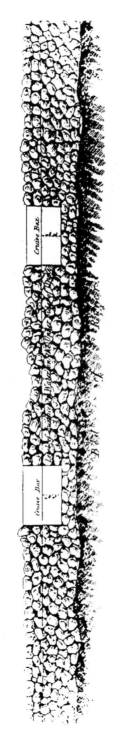

SECTIONS
of
CRUIVE DYKE
on
The River Don

Longitudinal Section of part of Dyke. shewing Cruive Boxes & Bed of River.

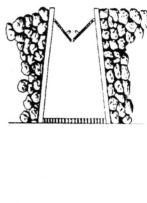

Plan of Cruive Box.

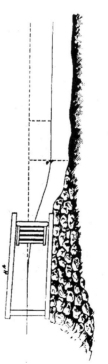

Section across Dyke. through Cruive Box

35 *Salmon cruive (from Report on Salmon Fisheries in Scotland.1836)*

only eels. So the Bishop's men got together eel nets from all sides, and threw them into the sea. By God's help they caught three hundred fish, of all different kinds.

A great deal of evidence for the consumption of fish has come from the excavation of middens of prehistoric times. A wealth of information can also be gleaned from manuscripts, carvings and other artefacts. By making use of these main areas of evidence we are able to deduce what varieties of fish were caught and consumed.

CRUIVES

Cruives were possibly the most sophisticated of the fishing methods used. A cruive consisted of a weir built most of the way across a river, with a number of small gaps left for wicker fish-traps, and one larger gap to allow the fish to pass upstream during the weekly and annual close times. The right to fish by this method could be operated only where there was an express Crown grant of cruive fishing and could only be used in that part of a river where there was no tidal movement. The use of cruives was carefully controlled, with the need for a free space to be left in mid-stream being particularly important. The law was surprisingly detailed. A twelfth-century law declares:

> *in sa mekill that ane swine of thre zeir auld and weill fed is of length, and may turn him within it, in sic ane manner that nather his grunzie [snout] nor his tail tuich ony of the sides of the cruives that are biggit on ilk side of the water.*

In other words, a well fed, three-year-old pig should be able to turn in the gap, so that neither his nose nor his tail could touch the ends of the dyke. The picture of members of the medieval peasantry trying to lower a squirming pig into a fast flowing river while perched between the dyke ends is a fascinating one. Presumably they took the easy way out and measured it first!

YAIRS AND STELLS

Yairs were another common method of catching salmon, more commonly used nearer the mouths of rivers in tidal flows. They were curved stone or wooden structures that ran out from the bank of the river and curved upstream to form an arc. Wooden stakes interwoven with wattle have been recorded in some yairs, which show complex wattle and stake features at intervals along their length. Other yairs have been recorded with zigzag plans, designed to trap fish on both the ebb and the flood of the tide.

A further method of trapping salmon was the Stell Net, in which

> *a long net is carried out into the sea and dropped in the form of a semicircle having its curvature toward the line of their approach, and one end of the net is fastened close to the land. A man seated on top of a rock or a pole descries their approach from a great distance and makes a signal when they enter the curve. Stones are thrown to scare the fish from escaping. Only floats support the net.*

36 *Yair near Kirkcudbright. (Copyright: The Stewartry Museum)*

Such 'fixed engines' in tidal waters were made illegal in the mid-nineteenth century. The word 'stell' originally meant a pool in the river where fish in earlier times could be trapped in the falling tide. It had meant an enclosure, and was also used to describe a sheep fank. Part of the South Esk opposite Montrose Harbour was known as the 'Stell' and is so marked on maps. It was gradually silting up by 1863, and with the building of the Sea Oil Base in the early 1970s, it disappeared altogether.

Net and Coble

The most common method of catching salmon for hundreds of years was the net and coble. It is still employed on many rivers, though no longer on the South Esk. This contraction of the industry is due partly to dwindling stocks caused by netting at sea, partly to the influence of fish farms. Perhaps a greater factor, however, in the demise of the wild salmon netting industry was the increase in the cost of equipment and wages in a labour intensive trade, without a parallel increase in the selling price of the end product. Whereas it had been possible up until the fifties to run a successful fishery on a catch of 500 salmon per annum, with the advent of fish farming, the industry became uneconomic.

Ungallant Knights

Written sources can also provide indirect evidence of fishing methods, both intentional and unintentional. One amusing example can be found in a courtly romance called *Fergus of Galloway, Knight of King Arthur* by Guillaume le Clerc, set in Scotland, and probably written

about 1200. A knight has been toppled into a river
by the hero at a joust and is mercilessly mocked:

> By my faith, sir, you're very bad mannered to
> fish in my river without my permission! Why,
> you have even made an eel-trap with your coat
> of mail! Let us keep a reckoning of what he has
> caught, for he must leave something for others
> to fish.

Whether a Frenchman, writing at that time,
would have had a detailed knowledge of
contemporary fishing practice in Scotland,
or merely projected his own experience, we do
not know. Nevertheless, this fascinating little

37 *Knight in the river*

episode tells us that even then, fish stocks were jealously guarded and permits were required
to fish. Nothing changes! We also learn that eels were commonly trapped, and in fact we know
that they were a prized commodity at the time. A charter by William the Lion to the monks of
Dunfermline Abbey grants them a tithe of the Royal eels caught in Fife.

38 *Drawing the nets. (Copyright: Penrose Lindsay)*

LEGAL REGULATION

The legal regulation of fishing in Scotland can be traced back at least 700 years, particularly as regards salmon fishing. The requirement for a weekly close time when no fishing for salmon is permitted, commonly known as the 'Setterday Slap', has been a feature of Scottish fisheries management from the time of Alexander II, or perhaps even his father, William the Lion, in the late-twelfth century. In 1424 James I brought in an Act 'anent the time quhilk Salmound suld nocht be slaine', which set out not only the weekly close time but the annual close season also – from the Feast of the Assumption (15 August) until the Feast of St Andrew (30 November).

MEDIEVAL TRADE

Although Montrose is thought to have received its royal charter about 1130, Scotland had only in the previous hundred years freed itself from Norse ascendancy at sea. Foreign traders had only begun to explore Scottish markets in the reign of Malcolm Canmore at the end of the eleventh century, mainly due to the influence of his wife, the saintly Margaret. Harbours, such as Montrose, or Stromnay as it then was, were the points of contact with a then largely unknown outside world, where Scotland 'plugged in' to these novel influences. These early burghs were populated in the main not by people from the local area, but by Scots-speaking craftsmen and artisans from the Lothians and Flemish speakers from Flanders, many with outgoing and entrepreneurial ideas.

As a result, in the twelfth and thirteenth centuries, the export of fish became increasingly important. The abundance of Scottish salmon fisheries at this time was proverbial in Spain and other parts of the Continent. As only tenants of David, Earl of Huntingdon, the King's brother, could trade through Dundee, and only the monks of Arbroath Abbey could trade through Arbroath, all remaining trade out of Angus and the Mearns passed through Montrose.

KING'S CADGER'S ROAD

In the reigns of Alexander II and III, salmon caught at the Usan nets were taken by a track known as the King's Cadger's Road from Usan to the King's table at Forfar. This must have been a valuable source of income to the Usan estate although the right to transport these fish and present them at the royal table was held by the Tulloch family of Bonnyton.

By the early-fourteenth century, despite many ups and downs, Montrose had become the second most important salmon exporting port in Scotland after Aberdeen. The ascendancy of the port as a salmon-exporting conduit was, unfortunately, rather short-lived, for a century later, in 1435, there was a decline in the salmon trade. This downturn was reflected in the export figures as only 87 barrels were shipped that year, all by Englishmen. However, from about 1525 onwards, the salmon trade was booming again, although trade as a whole through Montrose had declined.

Fishing on the South Esk and the Basin

The rights to fish any river in Scotland were originally vested in the King. These rights were then distributed to monasteries and the more powerful barons, and later to the developing burghs. Montrose's Charter from King David II in 1369 has been quoted above, granting the town fishing rights in both the North and South Esk.

As far as the South Esk fishings were concerned, records show only that the town was feudal superior for the north bank. Their writ ran from the Beany Bank at the entrance to the Basin to the Annat Bank at the seaward end. These beats were leased in 1463 for an annual render, or rental, of 51 salmon, the roll of fishers being made up by William Rynde of Montrose. The rights were jealously guarded, as salmon was a profitable commodity.

One of the earliest examples of the setting of 'tacks', or fishing leases, is recorded in the Montrose Head Court Book dated 24 February 1463. Here, the tacks were exposed to roup, or auction. Of the four tacksmen who were successful, one took a whole net at nine merks per year, and three took a half net each at four-and-a-half merks, all payable at Whitsunday and Martinmas. A merk was equivalent to 13s.4d. Scots, two-thirds of a pound, valuing a whole net at £6 Scots per annum.

The 'South Water Tacks' are next referred to in 1478, when they were further subdivided, being calculated in quarters. They were leased to four men, John Cruickshank, David Nanweik, Robert Ferrier and David Rukby, who were all burgesses of Montrose. The annual value of one quarter net was 20s. Scots on this occasion, representing, on the face of it, a drop in value of one third in only 15 years, though we cannot tell if the nets were of equal productivity or extent, and hence, worth.

There is evidence that the clergy were partly paid in kind, as George Gledstanes, minister at Montrose donated 'half of the teinds of the salmon fishing in the water of South Esk' to the magistrates of Montrose on leaving office in 1587.

Increasing Returns

Subdivision of tacks continued, and we find that in 1636, Alexander Erskine was tacksman for 'three tenth parts of the salmond fishings' in South Esk for John Erskine, Laird of Newbigging, later Provost. This amounted to £6 3s.4d. Scots. The remaining seven tenths was in possession of the Burgh.

Yet further fractioning took place, so that by the mid-seventeenth century the town fishings were feued in sixteenths. These ever-smaller portions speak of increasing profits, thus attracting those of an entrepreneurial turn of mind, in this case the Scotts of Rossie. By 1742 they held all sixteen sixteenths of Montrose's town fishings, in addition to their holdings on the south bank of the South Esk, and several tacks held by other members of the family on the North Esk. Revenue to the town was from tacks or feus only, and as these were long running, they tended to be devalued by inflation; so the town did not derive much financial benefit from them.

South Bank Fishings

By contrast, the fishings on the south bank of the Basin and river, certainly the most lucrative, have never belonged to the town. Like the rights held by the burgh, they were originally in the gift of the King. On 17 July 1542, King James V granted, inter alia, the fishings of South Esk at Kinnaird to Robert Carnegie of Kinnaird. The king was to die only five months later, a few days after the battle of Solway Moss. His daughter, Mary, Queen of Scots, confirmed the charter, including the fishing rights, on 25 March 1565.

While the life of James V ended in despair amid grim forebodings about the fate of his newly-born daughter, the Carnegie family went from strength to strength. On 10 November 1629, Robert Carnegie's descendant, the first Earl of Southesk, saw his daughter, Magdalen, married to a young man, James Graham, the fifth Earl of Montrose, later first Marquis, who was to be one of the most romantic and evocative figures in Scottish history.

As with many marriage contracts, as well as transfers of land, and other legal transactions of the time, the rights to salmon fishing were an important element. This marriage contract included life rent of

> all and haill the Lands and Barony of Auld Montrose, with the tours, fortalice, milnes, multures, salmond fishings of South Esk … the Lands of Marietown with aikeres thereof, and salmond fishing belonging to the said lands.

These 'Lands of Marietown', now known as 'Maryton', had featured 60 years earlier, in 1566, soon after the Reformation, when Alexander Campbell was Bishop of Brechin, a bishopric he had gained due to the patronage of his uncle, the fifth Earl of Argyll.

Perhaps by way of returning the favour, now that church lands were being 'liberated' as a result of the Reformation, he made over to his highly placed uncle church property in Farnell, and the whole of the lands of Maryton, with its salmon fishings.

Hard Times

The upheavals caused by the Covenanting Wars and the Civil War caused a shake-up in the fortunes of some local families. In particular, just after the Restoration, we find that the affairs of David Carnegie of Craig are in some disarray. On 14 September 1663, he found it necessary to unburden himself of part of his estate, which he did to the not inconsiderable tune of '£44,113 7s. and £2,249 14s.8d. as Sheriff's fee' to his kinsman Lord Lour. This disposal included most of the lands of Rossie, the lands and Barony of Usan, the ferry-boat at Montrose 'with the profits thereof', and that most important concomitant, the rights to salmon fishing.

Writing a few years later, in 1678, Rev Robert Edward emphasises the profusion of the catches:

> In the two Esks there are many thousands of salmon caught every season, sufficient not only to supply the inhabitants, but also merchants for exportation to foreign countries. During the season,

the common people kindle fires on the banks of the rivers (privately at night, because prohibited by the law), and while the fish flock to the light, they are pierced with spears and carried away.

The spears referred to were probably 'leisters' – small tridents still to be seen in fishing museums.

Meanwhile the Scotts were consolidating their grip on the South Esk fishings. In 1712, Alexander Beattie resigned his three-tenth parts of the salmon fishing in the South Esk in favour of Patrick Scott of Rossie. The Council accepted the change with alacrity ('immediately signed'), especially as the buyer offered to deliver to the Council or Magistrates 'in their name, the Town's Arms, handsomely cut in stone'.

The South Sea Bubble

Then, in 1720, the outside world impinged on these parochial concerns with a tempting offer. A letter was received by the Council from the pretentiously named Company of the Royal Fishery of England

> *acquainting them that their Company had allowed an additional subscription of £300,000 Sterling for the benefit of the Scots Nation, and that £3000 thereof was allowed to this Burgh'.*

The 'South Sea Bubble' was a mania of speculation which overtook all classes throughout the United Kingdom in the second decade of the eighteenth century, and led to the setting up of a large number of spurious companies, such as this one, in an attempt to 'make a killing'. The Company of the Royal Fishery of England had deigned to allow the citizens of Montrose to contribute £3000 to this folly. Even the Convention of Royal Burghs got in on the act, and intimation was made by 'touch of drum' (the contemporary equivalent of local radio) for persons to come forward and state how much they would 'adventure'.

Only 25 years previously, before the Union of the Parliaments, the Scots nation had almost been bankrupted by the failure of a similar get-rich-quick venture, the Darien Scheme. Perhaps for this reason the Council themselves were more canny. They did not put forward any funds, and the Scott family stepped in to the rescue. We read in the Council minutes that the Right of the 'Royal Fishings' belonging to the Burgh were in effect given to James Scott the Elder of Logie for finding the £3000 asked for. He was allowed to keep the fishing on handing over his receipt.

The Company of the Royal Fishery of England, along with 13 other 'bubbles', was suppressed in 1720, but not before many investors had 'ruined themselves with fantastic eagerness'.

Trade Unaffected

The bubble having burst and the commotion subsided, trade in salmon continued to prosper. The Scott family was still to the fore. In 1742 Archibald Scott of Rossie was exporting his own catches. He also traded salmon out of Inverness and Dunbar. Ships such as the locally owned

Success and the *Robert and Ann* could carry about 200 barrels of salmon, often to the Scottish staple port of Campvere in Flanders.

This old-established Scottish foothold among the low-lying coastal islands of what is now the Netherlands is known today as Veere. The privileged position of Veere in trading with Scotland began in 1444 when the local Lord of Veere married Mary Stewart, daughter of James I. In 1541 the town was officially recognised as the entrepot for Scottish exports such as salmon, wool and hides. Scottish merchants were given many privileges in the town such as freedom from taxation and their own church. The relationship did not come to an end until 1799. At the wharf can still be seen two ornate, burgher's houses called the '*Schotse Huizen*', gable-ends to the street, as in Montrose.

As the trade expanded, the smaller Scottish vessels had sometimes to be augmented by larger ships such as the *Midgatchen*, probably owned by Alexander Strachan of Tarrie, north of Arbroath, which took 1047 barrels of salmon from Montrose to Venice in 1746. Trade was obviously not to be interrupted by a minor and distant skirmish such as Culloden! By 1750, total exports of salmon from Montrose had risen to about 2400 barrels per annum.

39 *De Schotse Huizen, Veere. (Copyright: a3franke, Veere, The Netherlands)*

The Ministerial View

Not many years after this, parish ministers in Scotland were invited to describe their parish for that great undertaking known as the First Statistical Account. The minister at Craig, writing in the late 1780s, recorded that:

> The salmon Fishings on the South Esk belonging to two proprietors in this Parish [presumably Rossie & Usan] were formerly very prolific. Those of Rossie yielded 10,000 salmon and grilse, but since 1781 have fallen off greatly. A barrel of salmon sold 20 years ago for about 3 gns, but lately the prices have doubled.

His colleague at Maryton waxed lyrical rather than mathematical:

> On the river South Esk there is great plenty of fish – salmon, grilse, sea trout, finnocks, and a variety of river-trout. In the month of May, a prodigious quantity of beautiful, clear small trouts, called smouts [smolts] make their appearance ...

But as far as the mundane business of turning an honest penny from the trade in salmon was concerned, we have the testimony of another reverend gentleman, Mr James Headrick, who writes in 1813:

> Since Mr George Dempster of Dunnichen suggested the plan of conveying fresh salmon to the Capital, packed in ice, those who adopted this plan have realised princely fortunes, and the proprietors of salmon fisheries have obtained rents which may seem almost incredible. Every salmon fishery of any note is now provided with an ice-house.
>
> The salmon are packed in large wooden oblong boxes with pounded ice interposed betwixt them. They remain in the ice-house until they are removed on the smack. They are conveyed to London as fresh as when they came out of the water; and the ice which remains unmelted is used by confectioners.

Confections with a tang of fish were perhaps to the taste of Londoners at the time! These new-fangled arrangements operated to the disadvantage of local consumers, as only the poorer quality fish were sold at Montrose market. But the change did allow Mr Headrick to quote a well known saying:

> I remember when servants ... used to stipulate that they should not be obliged to eat salmon more than thrice in a week: but since this mode [packing in ice] was adopted, they are seldom troubled with them even once a year.

Stake Nets cause Disharmony

Stake nets began to be introduced around the turn of the nineteenth century. On the Rossie beats they were placed across the channel of the river opposite Craig, and at Rossie Mills.

But once again dissension arose, and the Carnegies at Kinnaird, proprietors of Old Montrose, perhaps visualising their rightful quarry being intercepted downstream, resorted to the law. Two 'bills of Suspension and Interdict' were presented in 1805 at the instance of Sir David

40 *Tending the nets. (Copyright: Penrose Lindsay)*

Carnegie, one against John Erskine of Dun, the other against Phillip Redpath of Berwick-on-Tweed, who was tacksman of the Rossie fishings, over the use of stake nets. This is almost the first instance we see of 'outsiders' holding tacks in the area, indicating the increased revenue to be got from salmon fishings after the beginning of the nineteenth century. Sir David died that year, but Dame Agnes Carnegie, his 'relict', pressed on with the action. (Although the word 'relict' sounds rather dismissive to our ears, it was the legally correct word at the time, and applied to widowers as well as widows.) The confusion caused by disagreement over the legal position was further confounded when the river disobligingly changed course during the 1820s.

In 1824 Sir James Carnegie of Southesk, then owner of the estate of Old Montrose, claimed that part of his land lay on the north side of the river The matter was eventually settled in Southesk's favour.

Berwick Men Infiltrate

By the beginning of the nineteenth century, outside firms were moving in to take over the ever more lucrative salmon trade, leasing tacks from local fishing estates such as Rossie, Dun, and Kinnaird, and controlling the process of netting, curing and exporting.

On 1 December 1800, the Rossie fishings were advertised for roup. They had been let for some years previously to Messrs Richardson of Perth, one of the earliest firms of 'incomers'.

The successful bidder was a Mr Hall of Berwick, who offered a yearly rent of £600. Many of these firms originated in Berwick, one such being Reidpath and Landells, who leased the Dun fishings in 1812, and probably owned a large ice-house which was built on Constable Hill in 1790.

Berwick firms spread to many parts of Scotland. Joseph Johnston and Sons, for many years an important presence in the area as fish-merchants and exporters, was founded by the son of the agent in Helmsdale for another Berwick merchant, who came south to Montrose in 1826.

METHODS OF CURING SALMON

Throughout the Middle Ages, the principal method of preparing salmon for export was to pack them in barrels after par-boiling and pickling in salt. Coopers hired by the tack holders did the packing. The quality or 'bind' of the fish, the exact capacity of the barrels, and the standard of packing, were obviously of great importance to the reputation of the town. In 1532 a lease stipulated that the salmon delivered were to be 'full reid and sweit and of the rycht bind of Montrose'.

Any dereliction of duty by the coopers was severely dealt with by the Council. A Parliament of James VI laid down the dimensions for barrels to be followed, and the 'haill cupery of the Burgh' was exhorted to comply. The Deacon of Coopers was presented with a standard barrel gauge in 1659 and ordered to 'conforme to the said gadge'. The barrels were branded with the mark of the port of origin, in the case of Montrose with a crowned 'M'. The Deacon of Coopers had custody of the branding iron. The barrels used for packing salmon were usually 42 gallons, although half-barrels are also noted. About 2 bushels of salt were required per barrel. This large amount explains the flourishing trade in salt. Packing in salt was superseded in the last 20 years of the eighteenth century by a method known as 'kitting', which involved pickling in vinegar and salt and packing in a tub which held 40 salmon. A local recipe survives for this from Margaret Scott, Lady Logie, from about 1775:

> Boil your salmond with a strong pickle of salt as usual, and after it is boiled take it from the pickle, lett it stand until cold, scume all the fat from the pickle and boil it with Jamaica pepper, a little black pepper, and a few bay leaves. When it is cold, take half of this pickle and half vinegar and putt over your salmond.

Kitting of salmon was soon overtaken by packing in ice, introduced by George Dempster of Dunnichen, as mentioned above, which held the field until the advent of refrigeration.

ANCILLARY TRADES

The trade in salmon could not have been carried on without the support of ancillary trades such as salt manufacturing and importing, barrel making, cotton spinning and boat building.

Salt pans were an early feature of the scene around Montrose Basin, being first mentioned in a charter granted to Jedburgh Abbey by King Malcolm IV between 1153 and 1160. These pans were probably at Old Montrose, but other saltworks are mentioned at Dun, where John de Hastings, having received the Barony of Dun from William the Lion in the twelfth century granted a saltwork and an acre of land from the estate to the monks of Arbroath Abbey.

In medieval times and later, one centre of production seems to have been at Saty Bank on the south side of the Basin, belonging to Rossie Estate, where the remains of the saltpans can still be seen. At Usan, a more substantial operation was built up at the end of the eighteenth century after a punitive tax on coal trade north of Redhead was removed.

Another saltwork is shown as 'saltings' on the east side of Montrose Basin, east of Tayock Burn and immediately south of the Brechin Road, on the 1924 OS Map. It may have been associated with the 'shambles' or slaughterhouse in the vicinity, as blood was used as a flux to remove impurities during the saltmaking process.

Unfortunately, Scottish salt was a rather dirty grey in appearance and met with considerable sales resistance as it was thought 'unfriendly to the human constitution' and unsuitable for fish curing. As a result there was a flourishing trade in Portuguese salt and 'Baysalt' from the Bay of Biscay. This was reflected in tradesmen's pay.

The Montrose Burgh Council meeting of 26 March 1765 fixed carters' wages at:

1   *for every load of great salt*   *2d*
      back or fore between the shore and any place in the town.

2   *for every load of small salt, excluding all meat and drink*   *2d*

3   *for each barrel of salmon, herring oil or tar or sack of flour*   *1d*

With the advent of ice as a preservative for salmon during transport, the need for salt diminished, though it was still used as a meat preservative and a condiment.

The Cooper's trade is an ancient one, and Montrose coopers claimed to have made the barrels for fish from the Marynett and the St Thomas Net on the North Esk to be transported to the Abbey of Arbroath and Brechin Cathedral. They were probably members of the Guild of Hammermen.

The earliest appearance of a member of the Cooper's Guild in the Town records is 1674. The raw material for barrels was usually oak, locally sourced, no doubt, in former times. By the eighteenth century, however, barrel staves were being imported from the 'Plantations', Virginia and Maryland, and from Riga and Danzig in the Baltic.

Joseph Johnston and Sons carried on cotton spinning for the manufacture of nets until superseded by synthetic fibres around 1970. They also had a boat-building yard in River Street in Montrose, as did Arbuthnott's, where they built cobles for their own use and for sale to other salmon fishing companies, some tailored to fit the requirements of particular fishing stations.

ANGLING

Fishing with a hook, or angle, has at least as long a history as fishing with a net. Fish hooks made of bone which are 20,000 years old have been found in Eastern Europe, and a very passable account of tying a fly was written by Claudius Aelianus in about AD250.

41 The Salmon Fisher *by William Lamb. (From the collections of the William Lamb Studio)*

Nearer to home, the first important mention of angling as a recreation rather than as a means of catching your dinner, was by one Dame Juliana Berners, Prioress of the Nunnery of Sopwell, near St. Alban's, 'a lady of noble family, and celebrated for her learning and accomplishments'. In about 1490, she wrote *A Treatyse of Fysshynge with an Angle*, which contains excellent woodcut illustrations of an angler with rod, line and float.

Izaak Walton's famous work, *The Compleat Angler*, has run to more editions than any other book except the Bible, a fact which recognises its literary merit as much as its appeal to fishers. It was published in 1653, two years after another equally valuable, but lesser-known work called *Barker's Delight, or the Art of Angling* which contains the first reference to a reel. From then until the nineteenth century, angling was the prerogative of landowners who were lucky enough to have rivers on their property and had the time and inclination to pursue the salmon and sea-trout. The coming of the railways hastened this process. In the area around Montrose Basin, the proprietors of the estates of Dun and Kinnaird were at various times keen anglers.

During the 1800s the development of Victorian sporting estates saw the creation of rod fisheries. The estate owners came to regard netsmen as detracting from their angling pleasure, and pushed them out to the coasts. This coincided with the formation of District Salmon Fishery Boards, which were established to protect and improve fisheries for salmon and sea-trout.

The setting up of local angling clubs, the principal of which is the Montrose and District Angling Club, founded in 1947, soon followed these developments.

MODERN TIMES

Those who made a living from the Basin in more recent times usually did so by working for the local salmon merchants. Within living memory, large numbers of sea-trout might be caught on one tide at the trout shot, Rossie Mills and the Log Bank. The fishers were paid 1*d*. per fish caught.

In the years before the Second World War, and for some time thereafter, the income of salmon fishers was supplemented by trapping and selling eels (for centuries a common activity on the Basin). The eels were boxed and sent to Billingsgate. Eel fishing was still commercially viable in the 1960s.

Scarts (cormorants) and sawbills (mergansers and goosanders) were considered vermin, as they were predators on the young salmon population. Local leaseholders of salmon tacks gave 2*s*.6*d*. per pair of feet. Seals, although less common, could make more serious inroads on the catch, and a pair of flippers would bring in 10*s*. to the kitty.

Wildfowling was another way of supplementing the rations. Geese and ducks were shot for the pot. What was then a way of augmenting the larder now continues as a much more circumscribed and regulated, but still popular, pastime.

42 Gathering Mussels *by William Lamb. (From the collections of the William Lamb Studio)*

9 'By Far the Most Extensive Mussel Beds in Scotland'

A History of Mussel Cultivation in Montrose Basin

A visitor to Montrose Basin at the end of the nineteenth century would have been forgiven for thinking that the area was an ideal one for the cultivation of mussels. A panorama lay before him of a large expanse of tidal flats extending to almost 1000 acres, divided at low tide by waterways into individual banks. These flats were a hive of industry at low water, dotted with mussel gatherers, many of them little more than children, bent under heavy baskets. They were home to 'by far the most extensive mussel beds in Scotland'.

This impression was, however, a misleading one. Montrose Basin is far from perfect for the propagation of mussels. Conditions may be more than adequate for growing young mussels, but well short of the optimum for the adults to breed. They often live where they can remain submerged at all times. Here, the water is shallow and the banks are high-and-dry at low tide. They are filtration feeders, and their own deposits of sifted mud accumulate, pushing them higher and higher out of the water. One bank in Montrose Basin is called the High Clay for this very reason. The circulation of nutrient-rich water is good, but whelks and starfish, the natural predators on mussels below water, are common. Their main enemies above the surface, oystercatchers and eider ducks, are among the most numerous inhabitants of the Basin.

In Scotland, mussels were not primarily articles of diet except in times of hardship. The eating of shellfish was much more of an English or Irish habit than a Scottish one. Sweet Molly Malone would have done scant trade had she wheeled her wheelbarrow, selling cockles and mussels, through the streets, broad and narrow, of Edinburgh or Montrose. They were all for bait rather than human consumption. There are records of the export of mussels from Montrose to many parts of Scotland, such as Portsoy and other small harbours along the Banffshire coast, and Peterhead, Dunbar, and Nigg among others. When the piping of sewage into the sea became widespread in the nineteenth century, many of the extensive English mussel beds, and some in Scotland, were polluted and destroyed.

MUSSELS BY THE MILLION

It is difficult nowadays to appreciate the huge numbers of mussels required to furnish the white fishing industry with bait for the 'small lines' – those catching mainly haddock and whiting. There are no figures available for Montrose, but at Eyemouth in 1887, the 40 boats fishing out of the port used no less than 91,770,000 mussels as bait costing an average of £66 per boat per annum, for a catch worth about £420. The cost of the bait was usually reckoned at about one eighth of the value of the catch, but this depended on whether it had to be imported, or was available close at hand, as in Ferryden, and hence without transport charges. Sometimes the total weight of fish caught at a fishing port was little greater, and quite often less, than the total weight of mussels (admittedly including the shells) used to catch them. The intensive labour involved in gathering or buying in, and setting the lines for such a mind-boggling number of shellfish can only be wondered at.

43 *James Johnston. (Copyright: Penrose Lindsay)*

Two dozen haddocks per week, and one cod fish

Inshore fishermen had used mussels as bait for many centuries. It was said that:

> *for the great lines used for cod and ling, herring and squid are used as bait, but for the small lines used for ordinary white fish … the mussel stands alone, and all others, however deadly, such as lugworm, herring, clams, cockles, limpets or bullock liver, must be considered as mere accessories.*

Up until the middle of the nineteenth century the natural powers of reproduction of *Mytilus edulis*, the edible mussel, had been quite sufficient to supply the needs of the white fishing community on the east coast of Scotland. But the advent of the railways, allowing rapid transport of the catch in good condition to centres of population in the south, caused such an increase in demand for bait for the 'sma' lines' that the mussel scalps were gradually depleted.

Changes in the techniques of fishing, and longer lines, also brought greater demand for bait. The cost of mussels as bait had doubled in the twenty years up to 1890.

A new initiative was clearly called for, and the man who provided that initiative was James Johnston, son of the founder of Joseph Johnston and Sons, 'Salmon Fishers and Mussel Merchants', of Montrose. It was only by dint of his very effective and painstaking research in the middle of the nineteenth century that the system of bed culture was introduced with so much success in Montrose Basin.

Dr J H Fullarton, a well known authority on shellfish at the time, wrote in the Annual Report for the Fishery Board for Scotland for 1889:

> Montrose Basin is a situation presenting great natural difficulties to the rearing of mature mussels. The success of mussel cultivation at Montrose is all the more apparent when it is contrasted with other places in Scotland where conditions are much more favourable, but only ruined beds are found.

In fact, conditions were so unfavourable that at Montrose mussels grew to only two inches even after three to five years' cultivation. This was not necessarily a disadvantage, however, as two smaller mussels were often preferred to one per hook, single large mussels being too heavy. In the same year, a report of the grandly named Scottish Mussel and Bait Bed Committee to 'the Most Honourable, the Marquess of Lothian KT, Secretary for Scotland', quoted James Johnston, no doubt calling on family memories, as saying:

> There was a time when seed was allowed to grow as it liked, and when fishermen got a boatload of mussels for £1 or 30s. It is a fact that the Ferryden fishermen were offered the Sands of Dun at the beginning of the century for £5 per annum, and two dozen haddocks per week and one cod fish, but bait was so cheap at the time that they did not think it worthwhile to take up the offer. These sands are now let to our firm at £500 per annum.

The Ferryden fishermen had obviously missed the boat on that occasion, but they were around to catch the next one, thanks to the ever-industrious James Johnston.

FERRYDEN AND USAN FISHERMEN'S MUSSEL SOCIETY

On 17 October 1853, at a meeting in Ferryden attended by all the line fishermen of the village, Johnston was instrumental in forming the Ferryden and Usan Fishermen's Mussel Society. Fullarton's report informs us:

> A week afterwards a meeting was held at Usan, when it was agreed to co-operate with the Ferryden men. The Society consisted of 144 members, 116 from Ferryden and 28 from Usan. Mr Johnston was appointed manager and treasurer, without fee.

Indignation was running high in the village at the time as five fisherwomen from Ferryden, 'whose character for honesty was unimpeachable', had recently been sentenced to imprisonment for three months for stealing mussels from the Dun beds. To add insult to injury, the crews of five Usan boats had just been apprehended on a similar charge, fuelling resentment against the landlords and sympathy for the fishermen. They did not need much persuading that a united voice, and the financial clout that went with it, were very much in their long-term interest. The ground on which the Society had fixed their hopes was the Salthouse Bank, to the south of the river channel, owned by Colonel Macdonald of Rossie and St Martin's. James Johnston was convinced it was possible to raise enough mussels there for the needs of the Ferryden and Usan 'sma' lines'.

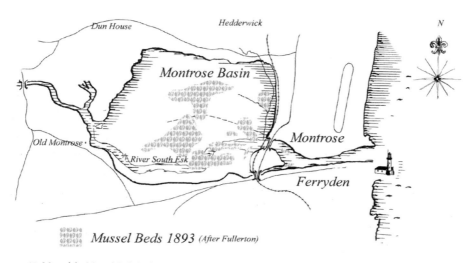

44 *Map of the Mussel Beds in the nineteenth century*

A great quantity of seed was obtained in the river and planted on the ground above the Salthouse Bank. Prior to 1853 there were no mussels on the Rossie ground: by 1890 it yielded about 600 tons a year.

ACCOLADE FOR JAMES JOHNSTON

Such outstanding success was worthy of national recognition and James Johnston was appointed to the Fishery Board for Scotland. Further praise was heaped upon his head in the committee report:

> *Montrose may be said to stand alone as affording a striking example of what can be effected by careful management, regulation and cultivation of mussel beds. The highest credit is due to Mr James Johnston of Montrose, not only for the enterprise and intelligence he has shown in the development of the beds in his own hands, but for the encouragement and assistance he has afforded to the local fishermen at Ferryden and Usan, who, at the instance of Mr Johnston, were induced to form and carry on the local association which leases and manages for the benefit of its members the beds on the south side of Montrose Basin.*

Not only did his well-researched methods allow previously unused ground to produce good crops of mussels, but the yield of existing beds was greatly improved. He adopted a 'gardening' system of sowing mussel seed, transplanting the growing mussels, and even 'weeding' them by removing predators such as whelks and starfish. Six or seven young boys were taken on in spring and summer to rid the Rossie beds of 'buckies', as whelks are known in many parts of Scotland. Three or four times a year, a concerted attack was made on them, and up to 120 women and children could be seen working together. Three or four cartloads were sometimes cleared at one tide.

However, as with all 'best laid plans', some difficulties had to be overcome. Insufficient mussel seed could be found in the Rossie ground or the Inch Burn, and neighbouring tacksmen were only too ready to take advantage of the situation.

COUNTER ATTACK FROM DUN

On the return of the boats from the herring fishing in 1855, when the Mussel Society had been in operation for only one full season, the tacksman of the Dun sands informed the Ferryden fishers that he could not provide a supply of mussels for the following season. This was a rather unsubtle attempt to destroy the work done by the Society up to then. He also wanted to buy up all the seed and mussels, no doubt offering an attractive price. The members of the Society took the advice of Mr Johnston and refused to sell. If they had sold, their preliminary work would have been destroyed.

But the rebuff had the effect that the men of Ferryden were forced back on their own devices, and had to do the best they could from their newly-acquired ground at Rossie. Unfortunately, being unfamiliar with the forbearance required in nurturing mussels on new beds, they carried on with their time-honoured practices, selling what mussels they could gather without regard to their maturity. This resulted in the beds 'being impoverished by them gathering three times as many as they required'. The Mussel Society having got off to a rather rocky start, the guiding hand of James Johnston once again held the ship steady, and the Rossie beds were divided into four areas corresponding to the year of planting, thus allowing harvesting in rotation only of mature mussels.

GOING DUTCH

Despite the sterling efforts made by the Mussel Society, led by James Johnston and James West, the Mussel Manager, they had by no means a clear field in the supply of mussels to the Ferryden fishermen. The quality of the bait taken from Montrose Basin, due to its prolonged period of growth, was poorer than that of some imported competitors. In addition, despite the great distances they had to be transported, they do not seem to have been at a disadvantage on price. A letter from William Mair, the Fishery Officer at Montrose to the Fishery Board for Scotland in 1897 stated:

𝕸inute of 𝕸eeting at 𝕱erryden,

7ᴛʜ JULY, 1894.

Saturday, at 7 o' Clock evening.

AT a full Meeting of the Fishermen of Ferryden, publicly called by bell, the following Resolutions were agreed to after a statement made by Mr. JAMES JOHNSTON, Mr. ALEX. MEARNS, Jr., Mr. JAMES WEST, for himself and Committee of Ferryden Fishermen, who were in London, their names being :—

> WILLIAM MEARNS, (King).
> JAMES WEST, Mussel Manager.
> WILLIAM COULL, Barnat's Willie.
> JOHN PATON, Mettlie.
> JAMES PERT, Prod.
> ALEX. SUMMERS.
> ALEX. PERT, Collie's Sie.

That the Committee should sign, on behalf of the Fishermen, a cash credit in the Montrose Branch of the National Bank of Scotland for the amount of the expense of the Provisional Order ; that the Fishcurers pay 1d. per barrel on their last year's exports ; that the money already contributed and in the hands of the Committee be paid over to this Fund ; that the contribution of £25 by Mr. George Stevenson, of Messrs. Forbes, Stuart, & Coy., London, be also applied ; and that Funds be raised in future till the Debt is discharged as follows :—

1. That every Herring Boat in Ferryden and Usan pay for this season as soon as possible 15s. per boat.

2. That on and after 1st September, 1894, 1d. per box be collected by Fishcurers, Fish Salesmen, and others, and after the dues of 1s. per ton is paid to the Harbour Trustees, the balance to go for the liquidation of the Debt.

3. That in years to come, until the Debt is paid, ½d per cran shall be paid, beginning with the Herring Fishing season of 1895.

4. That if necessary 1d. per measure be paid on each measure sold off the grounds of the Ferryden and Usan Mussel Society.

5. That the Debt be extinguished not later than the last legal day of December, 1899.

And that an excerpt of this Minute of Meeting be signed by Mr. JAMES JOHNSTON and Mr. JAMES WEST, and a copy given to the National Bank Agent at Montrose, and also printed copies circulated among Fishermen.

45 Minute of Meeting at Ferryden *showing bye-names in use*

Dutch mussels and mussels from the South Esk are practically the same price delivered, any difference in cost being in favour of those from Holland. The Dutch mussels are uniformly of good quality, well-filled, clean and large, one mussel to a hook. South Esk mussels, on the other hand, are not of such uniformly good quality nor so large as the foreign mussels. … the Dutch mussels are considered to fish best, and the fishermen prefer them.

But supplies from Holland were seasonal. Mr Mair's letter continues:

> *Mussels are imported from Holland in the late Autumn and early Spring months. The supply is cut off in mid-Winter by frost, and from April onward the weather is too mild to risk their importation.*

Steamers bringing mussels from the Low Countries might call as many as eight times during the autumn, landing more than half their cargo at Montrose, afterwards going on to Stonehaven, Peterhead, Fraserburgh, Buckie, and Macduff. Imports were also made from Morecambe Bay, Boston in Lincolnshire, and Ireland at various times at least until the 1920s. In 1916, one of Mr Mair's successors, Frederick Fraser, became involved in a dispute between the Mussel Society and Montrose Harbour Board, who claimed the right to the mussels in the South Esk from the Suspension Bridge to Scurdie Ness. In support of their claim, they produced a charter, translated from the Latin, and backed it up with a poster. Mr Fraser was scathing in his dismissal of the Harbour Board's case.

> *The translation of the charter from Latin into English was, I should state, done by the Harbour Clerk. In my opinion the terms are not quite explicit enough as no specific reference is made to the Trust's right to the mussel fisheries. The Harbour Board never bestowed any attention on the mussel beds in question.*

Two months later, Mr Fraser reported that the Harbour Board were leaving the matter in abeyance until word was received from the Fishery Board for Scotland. But in the meantime, the dredgers were reluctantly paying landing dues of 1s.8d. per ton, which was considered an exorbitant charge, as white fish were charged 1s.3d., and coals only 4d. per ton.

46 *Sheelin' mussels. (Copyright: Angus Council Cultural Services)*

47 *Daily activities in Ferryden. (Copyright: Angus Council Cultural Services)*

THE FISHERWIFE'S LOT

The life of a fisherman may have been hard, but his wife's lot was just as arduous. Her day began with the shelling (or sheelin') of the mussels, using a sheelin' knife, then setting (baiting) a line of 1200 hooks with two mussels on each hook. It was a monotonous and laborious task which took about two hours per line, not counting the time required for sheeling. Sometimes two lines had to be baited for each member of the crew. She was occasionally helped by her husband provided he was not at sea, and he had a mind to. In addition, weather conditions were liable to rapid change, so their painstakingly baited lines might have to be discarded.

As the line was baited, it had to be coiled very carefully into a line-creel, or scull, the coils separated by grass cuttings or newspaper (the *Daily Express* being greatly favoured) to prevent snagging when it was paid out at sea. The children were involved in the gathering of mussels and also the sheelin', being required to clean a certain number before they went to school. The job of redding, or clearing the used lines of seaweed, starfish, unused bait and other rubbish, followed by setting them with the new bait, was done inside the house in winter, and outside, to the relief of all, when the weather improved.

The stench may not have lessened, however, as Ferryden was well known for the shell-middens which obstructed the side alleys and even the main streets. By the end of the nineteenth century, these middens were disappearing, their contents ground down and used as fertiliser. The fisherwife, having completed her task with the lines, continued with her daily darg. She cleaned the house, cooked the meals, washed the clothes, and brought up the

48 *A typical fishwife 1888. (Copyright: Angus Council Cultural Services)*

children. She also had to go out to the mussel scaups to gather the bait, often accompanied by her children, and trudge back, with laden baskets called 'murlins', fore and aft.

The man of the house, while working very hard while at sea, was happy to take his ease if possible, while on terra firma. One historian of Ferryden, writing of the 1830s said:

> *It was the custom at this time for a husband, when he had anything particular to say to his wife, to go to the public house, whence he would send for his better half, and after due ceremony, point out to her, in the full hearing of all present, whatever his lordly mind was charged with.*

Little wonder that fishermen's wives were almost always daughters of other local fishing families. Nevertheless, their hard lives reflected centuries-old traditions.

'A Bait of Musselt'

The first reference to mussels in the Montrose Council records is in the Treasurer's Account in 1470, where one 'Walter' is unwilling to take on a charge of 8s.4d. due to John Anderson by David Wrycht for a 'bait of musselt'. The reason for his refusal is unclear. A much more serious dissension occurred twenty years later, when on 16 September 1493, the good burghers of Montrose petitioned King James IV against John Erskine, third Laird of Dun, accusing him that:

> on Sanct Nineanis Day last bypast, quhare our fischers, their wyffis and seruandis were gadarende [gathering] their bait in your watter, as they haf done sene your saide burgh was fundit and antecedit, he sends his folkis and spulzeit [plundered] thaim of their claithes and withhouldes the samyn.

This dastardly deed was said to have happened on the back sands, on the west side of the Tayock Burn, on ground belonging to the Laird of Dun, so he no doubt felt justified in depriving the worthy fishers, and their wives and servants, of their clothes, leaving them exposed to the elements. Their rather querulous petition resulted in the issue of a royal warrant by James IV to 'our Scherof of Forfare' to serve a 'summons of spulyie' in the case of the Burgh of Montrose vs. Erskine of Dun.

All appears to be quiet on the mussel front for the next 200 years, or at least no problems arise serious enough to be brought to the notice of the Council. However, bickering is evident from the burgh records of 1711, when Patrick Renny of 'Ulysseshaven' or Usan complained that two of his boats were arrested by the town treasurer for 'away taking mussels'. On this occasion, the Council seem to have accepted responsibility, and the Treasurer, George Caldcleuch, was directed to make a payment of five shillings 'to discharge the arrangements on the boats'. But six years later in 1717, the jealously-guarded mussel beds are again brought to the unwelcome attention of the council when they receive a complaint that:

> The boats of Ferryden go on the West Sands and other places belonging to the town and do gather mussels.

This time there is no compromise and the Council instructs an officer grandly titled 'Collector of the Mussel Dues' to seize what mussels have been improperly gathered. There were frequent disputes throughout the eighteenth and nineteenth centuries among landowners and with the fishermen of Ferryden who used copious quantities for baiting their lines for haddock and cod. As the continued harvesting of the mussels took its toll on their powers of reproductive recovery, the council sought to prevent one of their prime assets being severely compromised. In a move reminiscent of present-day attempts to preserve stocks of cod and haddock, in 1765 the council stated that:

> considering the constant dregging of the mussels, the seed or young mussels are in danger of being quite lost, and issued a proclamation through the town by Drum, prohibiting the dregging of any mussels, also the selling of any mussels to strangers for one year.

49 Loading the Coble *by William Lamb. (From the collections of the William Lamb Studio)*

The prohibition on sale to strangers implies that fishermen from coastal villages such as Johnshaven, Gourdon, Usan, Auchmithie, and possibly further afield, were in the habit of using mussels from Montrose Basin. However, the interdict did not last long, being lifted the very next year. Either the mussels made a very rapid recovery, or the town coffers were in need of replenishment!

Further temporary bans on overtaxing the mussels were issued in the following forty years, until, in 1805, a dispute arose between two pillars of local society, Hercules Ross of Rossie, and a Mr Erskine, possibly John the fifteenth Laird of Dun. Mr Ross stated that for 100 years Montrose, through the tack to Rossie, had exercised the sole right of selling all mussels harvested in the South Esk. Mr Erskine's exclusive claim to the scalps could not stand. Matters became rather heated and Mr Erskine's writings were dismissed as 'trash'. Rossie stoutly defended his interests and he fired off another salvo to the Council only three days later warning the Council against the 'subtle arguements' of Erskine laying claim to the mussel beds. We have no mention in the burgh papers of Erskine's side of the story. However, the burgh eventually lost control of the beds in 1819 by a decree in favour of Miss Alice Erskine of Dun. A successful action was brought in 1818 by Miss Erskine against the Town Council, the fishers of Ferryden and others, in regard to the right of mussel gathering on Dun's ground in Montrose Basin, known as the Lands of Sands.

So was ended a connection between the people of the town, represented by the Council, and the collection of mussels, which stretched back probably to the founding of the burgh of Montrose in the twelfth century.

50 *Early Devonian scene, after Trewin and Davidson*

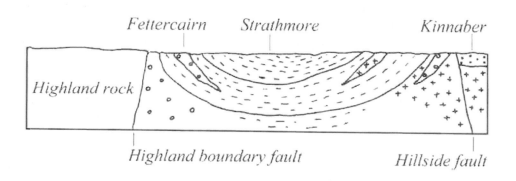

 Upper old red, Montrose Basin

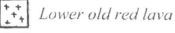 Lower old red lava

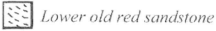 Lower old red sandstone

Lower old red conglomerate

51 *Geological section through North Angus*

10   The Geology of Montrose Basin

To appreciate the time-scale of the formation of Montrose Basin requires us to comprehend vast aeons of time.

The creation of the Basin involved events spread over 400 million years. These events occur in two separate episodes. The earlier was the time of formation of the solid rocks which underlie and flank the Basin during the Devonian Period of geologic time, which occurred about 400 million years ago. It was the pattern of soft and hard rocks from that time which determined the position of the Basin. The erosion of a low-lying area between higher ground took place in the Quaternary Period which covers the most recent one-and-a-half million years.

HIGHLAND BOUNDARY FAULT

Old Red Sandstone is the name given to one of the main rock-types from the Devonian Period. They are seen in a broad band which stretches across Scotland from Stonehaven in the north-east, to the Firth of Clyde. Southwards it extends through Angus to Fife. The northern margin forms the Highland Boundary Fault, which crosses Scotland from just north of Stonehaven, through Clattering Brig, the bottom of the Angus Glens, Dunkeld, Aberfoyle, Balmaha, the tip of Cowal, Bute and disappears in north Arran. North-west of this Fault in the Devonian Period lay a high mountainous region, while to the south-east was a valley which collected the sediment carried by rivers from the mountains. As much as 9km depth of sediment was deposited.

Overall the landscape was similar to that of the present day western USA. High mountains with an abrupt scarp at the margin drained by rivers; the lower valleys semi-arid, but irrigated in the vicinity of the rivers. These are found in many semi-arid regions of the world.

MONTROSE VOLCANIC FORMATION

The main rock formation found around Montrose is the Montrose Volcanic Formation, composed mainly of lava flows of a dark-coloured rock, locally known as 'Scurdie Rock'. It is well displayed on the foreshore between Ferryden and Scurdie Ness and forms Rossie Braes and the high ground of Hillside. Individual lava flows can clearly be seen in the cliffs below St Cyrus. The top and base of the flows are uneven and rubbly due to the breaking of the lava into blocks as it flowed, but the centre of each flow is massive. Small holes known as vesicles are common, formed by gases released by the pressure decrease as the lava flowed on the surface. Later hot volcanic water enriched in dissolved material deposited minerals in these spaces. Best known are the rhythmically banded silica nodules described as agate, for which the Formation is famed.

52 Climatius, *a fossil fish from Upper Silurian times*

FOSSIL FISH

Another local rock type formed the deposits from the alluvial valley floor. It is mainly sandstone and flagstones, but also includes at least one thin laminated unit laid down in a lake – the 'Fish Bed'. Good specimens of fossil fish are restricted to it. Recent excavations at Tillywhanland, by Forfar, have re-located the Fish Bed there.

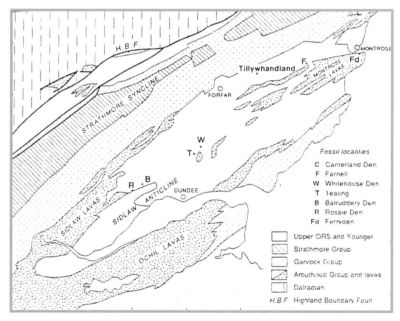

53 *Fossil beds in the Montrose area, after Trewin and Davidson*

A nationally important collection of fossils is held in Montrose Museum. Among them are primitive fish without jaws and teeth with the head flattened and heavily armoured by a bony carapace, while the remainder of the body is more streamlined and less-protected. The interior of the skull preserves detail of the brain and blood vessel structure within the head. These fish are similar to the modern lamprey.

Jawed fish, very distantly related to modern forms are also found. Many different species have been described from the area. These are small, streamlined organisms, covered in scales, and with sharp dorsal spines. Creatures distantly related to spiders were also found.

In addition to these body fossils, there are also trace fossils, indicators of animal activity rather than actual fossils. The best specimens have been collected from sediments in the Montrose Volcanic Formation, though they have been found elsewhere. At St Cyrus, vertical burrows have been found; at Ferryden Farm the trace fossils include sinuous trails of many feet, others with a central spine; still others show multiple legs and in some cases the marks of tail spines. All plants are primitive forms. They were small with upright stems and lived at water margins. A distinctive form is the enigmatic *Parka decepiens*, an oval shape with an internal polygonal structure. To the Victorian quarrymen it was 'puddock spawn'.

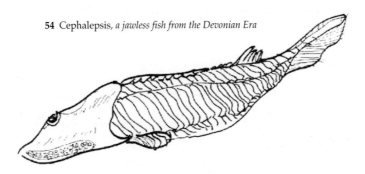

54 Cephalepsis, *a jawless fish from the Devonian Era*

A 350 MILLION YEAR GAP

No solid rocks younger than the Upper Old Red Sandstone, the soft rocks which underlie the Basin, are now present in the area. Thus there is a gap of over 350 million years in the geological history of the area. Not until the time of glaciation can the story be continued, and even this is almost entirely from the latter part of the period, since later glacial movement tends to erode earlier deposits. The earliest features from this era may include marine rock platforms and cliff lines. At Stonehaven the offshore rock platform is older than 2 million years in age, and platforms elsewhere along the coast may be inherited rather than post-glacial in origin. The area of low ground on which Montrose stands, situated in the readily erodable Upper Old Red Sandstone, contrasting with the higher ground of the area, is also likely to have been present in pre-glacial times.

CLIMATIC DETERIORATION

A world-wide deterioration of climate occurred 1·8 million years ago leading to the spread of ice sheets into middle latitudes. These glacial episodes were separated by warmer periods when the ice retreated. Cycles of differing climatic conditions occurred in Scotland, here listed in order of decreasing severity, with the modern equivalents in brackets: continental sheet ice when the entire area was under ice except for the highest mountain peaks (central Greenland); valley glaciers in mountain areas (high Alps); permafrost (northern Russia or Canada); wet temperate (Scotland); warm dry temperate (southern England).

GLACIERS

There were a number of glacial episodes. The last main glaciation ended 13,000 years ago, though a resumption of cold conditions with valley glaciers returned, with final melting at 10,500 years. Subsequently the climate has alternated between warm dry and wetter conditions. When the ice melts it floods the land, but the land rises much more slowly when released from the weight of the ice. The result is an oscillation between dry land and shallow seas in coastal regions.

THE COASTLINE BEFORE THE BASIN

The rise in sea-level formed a beach, which has now been raised above sea-level. It has resulted in a series of cliffs and beach deposits behind the present strandline best seen at St Cyrus, where it forms a prominent cliff. When the ice melted, the Basin area was an open bay, with arctic flora and fauna. It was a weakly saline estuary with a small peninsula at Maryton. The South Esk, Pow Burn and Tayock Burn had small deltas at their entries. The bay stretched as far back as Farnell. Fossils found are typical of estuaries of the present day. An important collection of these is in Montrose Museum.

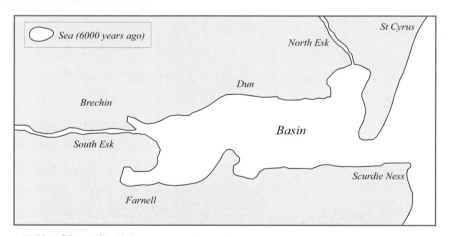

55 *Map of the coastline 6000 years ago*

TSUNAMI

An unusual event which occurred about 7000 years ago was the interruption of sedimentation by a thin sand layer containing marine plankton. This has been ascribed to a tsunami (tidal wave) caused by a major rock slip off the coast of Norway. Deposits from this momentous event have been found not only at Montrose Basin, but at other points on the east coast of Scotland as far apart as Sullom Voe in Shetland, and Dunbar in the south. Evidence of backwash from the wave has been found in Norway, where the bones of nine-month-old cod found in the deposits reveal the time of year the tsunami overwhelmed the coast. At the present day, cod spawn in the North Sea mainly in March, putting the inundation about mid-winter. The wave in the Montrose Basin area was 5–10 metres high. Peat deposits near the tsunami bed have been dated to a time when Mesolithic hunter-gathers were living in Scotland. Any Mesolithic inhabitants would have been vulnerable while foraging for shellfish along the coast. The sudden arrival of a 30ft wave without warning would have been catastrophic. Two inundated hunting camps have been found close to the Fife coast.

The sudden movement of water left a thin bed of sand rich in fossils from below the tide line. The identification of this as a tidal wave deposit is due to the numerous small plankton fossils characteristic of open water which would not normally be found along a shore line. They must have been swept in from offshore and stranded.

THE FORMATION OF THE PROMONTORY OF MONTROSE

The presence of two rivers in the bay caused considerable build up of shingle and longshore drift between them. A major series of spits built up eventually closing off the bay. In the Kinnaber area they are low with a complicated pattern. In the town they form the ridge of the High Street. The build-up of the promontory proceeded from east and west, resulting in the Clay Hauf, where the Basin muds and silts were deposited, and the Sandy Hauf where blown sand built up the Links. These persist to the present. The basin deposition is typically estuarine with silt, mud and shell banks which are dark and oxygen-poor. The river and its tributaries cut through these. On the east side sand has built up in series of dunes through the town, Mid Links, East Links to the present beach area. Sediment movement continued throughout the historical period, with deposition and erosion alternating.

The process continues!

56 *Montrose between Basin and sea*

Epilogue

The Basin in the Twentieth and Twenty-first Centuries

By the twentieth century the Basin had long ceased to be of any maritime importance but until the later part of the period it remained an important area for fishing and mussel farming, although there is now no longer any commercial activity on it.

Around the middle of last century the possibility of re-claiming areas of the Basin was raised again together with a counter proposal to completely flood the area so that it was perpetually full, to provide a marina and water-sports complex. Neither suggestion was ever acted upon.

The Basin had always been an important centre for wading and migrating birds as well as flora and fauna, and as a result the Wildlife Centre was built to provide, literally a focal point.

For the time being the Basin continues to be used by the sailing enthusiasts, the wildfowlers and the birdwatchers, with the needs of mankind balanced with those of nature.

The future of the Basin seems to be secure, and, for the foreseeable future at least, the tide will continue to ebb and flow through it, just as it has done for several thousands of years.

Bibliography

Adam, C E (ed) *View of the Political State of Scotland in the Last Century* (Edinburgh, 1887)

Adams, D G *Celtic & Medieval Religious Houses in Angus* (Brechin: Chanonry Press, 1984)

Adams, D G *Report on Salmon Fishing in the Montrose Area to 1835* (Typescript, 1985)

Adams, D G *Usan or Fishtown of Ullishaven* (Brechin: Chanonry Press, 1991)

Adams, D G, G Jackson & S G E Lythe (eds) *The Port of Montrose: a history of its harbour, trade and shipping* (Wainscott, NY: Georgica Press; Tayport: Hutton Press, 1993)

Adams, D G (ed) *Recepts worth While to Keep: an 18th-century Scots kitchen* (Balgavies, Angus: Pinkfoot Press, 2001)

Atkinson, N K *Hedderwick* (Typescript, 1990)

Atkinson, N K *The Early History of Montrose* ([Forfar]: Angus Council Cultural Services, 1997)

Bardgett, F G *Scotland Reformed* (John Donald Publishers, 1989)

Collins, G *Great Britain's Coastal Pilot* (1693)

Cook, M, & R Manzi *Reading a Burgh Archive:* the Montrose work book (Montrose: M Cook & R Manzi, 1994)

Davidson, F *An Inventory of the seventeenth century Tombstones of Angus* (Arbroath, 1977)

Donaldson, G *Scottish Church History* (Scottish Academic Press, 1985)

Dickinson, W C (ed) *History of the Reformation in Scotland by John Knox*

Dorward, D *The Glens of Angus: names, places, people* (Balgavies, Angus: Pinkfoot Press, 2001)

Douglas, A *History of the Village of Ferryden* 2nd ed (Montrose, 1857)

Edwards, D H *Among the Fisher Folks of Usan & Ferryden* (Brechin, 1921)

Fairfax-Blakeborough *The History of Horse Racing in Scotland*

Fraser, W *History of the Carnegies, Earls of Southesk and of their kindred* (Edinburgh, 1867)

Fraser, D *East Coast Oil Town Before 1700* (Montrose: Standard Press, 1974)

Fraser, Rev W R *St Mary's of Old Montrose or Parish of Maryton* (Edinburgh, 1886)

Hall, H *History of Montrose Water Supply from its Commencement in 1720 to 1914* (Montrose: Montrose Town Council, 1914)

Jacob, V *The Lairds of Dun* (London, 1931)

Jervise, A *The History and Traditions of the Land of the Lindsays in Angus and Mearns* (Edinburgh, 1853)

Jervise, A *Memorials of Angus and the Mearns* 2 vols (2nd ed, Edinburgh: David Douglas, 1885)

Fordun, John of *Chronicle of the Scottish Nation* W F Skene (ed) (facs repr 2 vols, Lampeter: Llanerch Publishers, 1993)

Johnson, G *Craig, Angus 1788+1791* (Aberdeen: Aberdeen & North East of Scotland Family History Society, 1986)

Kemp, D W (ed) *Tours in Scotland 1747, 1750, 1760 / by Richard Pococke ...* (Edinburgh, 1887)

Low, J G *Memorials of the Church of St. John the Evangelist ...* (Montrose, 1891)

Low, J G *Industry in Montrose: the kindred industries of Montrose* (?Dundee: Pitnolen Publications, 1994)

Lynch, M *Scotland: a new history* (London: Century, 1991)

Lynch, M (ed) *The Oxford Companion to Scottish History* (Oxford: Oxford University Press, 2001)

Macneill, W A *Montrose Before 1700 from original documents* (Dundee: Abertay History Society, 1961)

Mitchell, A *Pre-1855 Gravestone Inscriptions in Angus* 4 vols (Edinburgh: Scottish Genealogy Society, 1979-84)

Mitchell, J *The History of Montrose* (Montrose, 1886)

Morrison, D, & A I Mouat *Montrose Old Church: a history* (Montrose: Montrose Old Church Bicentenary Committee, 1991)

Moss, M *The 'Magnificent Castle' of Culzean and the Kennedy Family* (Edinburgh: Edinburgh University Press, 2002)

Murray, V *High Society: a social history of the Regency Period, 1788–1830* (London: Viking, 1998)

Nicolaisen, W F H *Scottish Place-Names: their study and significance* (new edn, Edinburgh: John Donald, 2001)

Ross, D *Scotland: history of a nation* ([Edinburgh]: Lomond Books, 1998)

Salter, M *The Castles of Grampian & Angus* (Malvern: Folly Publications, 1995)

Stansfeld, J *The Story of Dunninald* (William Culross, 1999)

Valentine, T *Old Montrose* (Ochiltree: Stenlake, 1997)

Warden, A *Angus or Forfarshire, the land and people, descriptive and historical*, 5 vols (Dundee, 1880-85)

Watson, W J *The History of the Celtic Place-names of Scotland* (Edinburgh, London: Blackwood & Sons, 1926; facs rep, Edinburgh: Birlinn, 1993)

West, J *A Personal History of Ferryden* ([?]Montrose: The author, 1988)

Will, C P *Place Names of Northeast Angus* (Arbroath, [1964])

Other Sources

Montrose Basin Heritage Society has developed an extensive research collection of information on sites and buidings around the Basin. Together with photographs, copies of historic maps and other documents, these sources have been used in the compilation of this book.

Key reference texts are listed below.

Angus Local Studies Centre:
    Montrose Burgh Council Minutes
    Montrose Burgh Head Court Book
    The Montrose Review
    The Montrose Standard
    The Brechin Advertiser
    Census Records
    Registry of the Great Seal of Scotland
    The First Statistical Account of Scotland 1793
    New Statistical Account of Scotland 1833
    Montrose Races MS 31
    Scott of Commieston Family Papers MS 463
    Valuation Rolls
    Acts of Parliament of Scotland

National Archives of Scotland:
    The Register of Sasines Tax Records
    National War Museum of Scotland
    National Portrait Gallery of Scotland

General:
    Burke's Landed Gentry
    House of Commons Research Paper 1999; 'The Purchasing Power of the Pound 1758–1998'
    Minutes of the Montrose Club, with kind permission of Mrs Dorothy Bruce-Gardyne
    Private papers by kind permission of the Earl of Southesk
    The Frick Collection, New York

Index

Montrose Basin Heritage Society

www.montrosebasinhistory.org.uk

Notes

The Pinkfoot Press

Balgavies, Forfar, Angus DD8 2TH

inbox@pinkfootpress.co.uk